The Art of Hilda Carline *Mrs Stanley Spencer*

Alison Thomas

The Art of HILDA CARLINE

Mrs Stanley Spencer

Edited by Timothy Wilcox

With a foreword by Frances Spalding

Lincolnshire County Council

Usher Gallery · Lincoln · in association with

Lund Humphries Publishers

London

Published on the occasion of the exhibition
The Art of Hilda Carline: Mrs Stanley Spencer
Usher Gallery, Lincoln *16 January – 7 March 1999*
Royal Albert Memorial Museum, Exeter *13 March – 7 May 1999*
Kenwood House, London, English Heritage *15 May – 11 July 1999*
York City Art Gallery *24 July – 29 August 1999*
Glynn Vivian Art Gallery, Swansea *11 September – 7 November 1999*

Exhibition curated by Timothy Wilcox and Alison Thomas
and jointly organised by the five venues.

Grant-aided by The Arts Council of England

First published in 1999 by
Lincolnshire County Council, the Usher Gallery
in association with Lund Humphries Publishers
Park House, 1 Russell Gardens, London NW11 9NN

British Library Cataloguing in Publication Data
A catalogue record for this book is available from the British Library

ISBN 0 85331 776 3

Designed and typeset in Adobe Jenson by Dalrymple
Printed in Belgium by Snoeck-Ducaju & Zoon, Ghent

Distributed in the USA by Antique Collectors' Club
Market Street Industrial Park, Wappingers Falls, NY 12590, USA

Front cover: *Self-portrait* 1923 (cat.39)
Frontispiece: Hilda Carline, Hampstead 1919
Back cover: *Swans, Cookham Bridge* c.1929
(cat.45)

CONTENTS

FOREWORD

This exhibition is to be welcomed. Hilda Carline is one of the most haunting figures in twentieth-century British art. Each time Stanley Spencer is hailed afresh as one of our greatest painters, some reference is usually made to the sad history of his marital relations. Hilda was Spencer's first wife, a complex woman with her own aspirations as an artist. Her strength of personality is evident in her drawn and painted self-portraits. But the conflicts within her, exacerbated by marriage to an indefatigable worker and talker, appear to have benighted her life. When Stanley developed a sexual fascination with Patricia Preece and conceived the notion of having two wives, the marriage with Hilda fell apart. Yet neither divorce nor wrangling over money nor her mental breakdown could destroy the extraordinary relationship that bound Spencer to Hilda, as Alison Thomas movingly describes in the catalogue essay. Spencer went on writing letters to Hilda even after she died.

But it is not only the intensity of her relationship with Spencer that makes Hilda a haunting figure. Some years ago her full-length portrait of the maid Elsie Munday was shown for the first time at the Anthony d'Offay Gallery in London and made a striking impression on all who saw it. It had strength and generosity, and a breathtaking forthrightness. How many other paintings did she produce with such confidence and panache? Or was this a rare moment in her career? When the Tate Gallery acquired a self-portrait of Hilda, it too caught attention and raised further questions. How does Hilda Carline relate and compare as an artist to Stanley Spencer and to the work of her two brothers Richard and Sydney Carline? These and other issues can now be examined in the light of this show.

My own interest in Hilda Carline began many years ago when I was invited to tea by Richard Carline at the family home in Hampstead. Stepping inside the house was like stepping into history, for the walls were crowded with paintings, by the father George Carline as well as by his three painter-children, also by Stanley Spencer, Henry Lamb and others. But it was the overall atmosphere of the house that was so memorable, weighted as it was by a mood that was slightly melancholy and austere. Having now read Alison Thomas's essay I can imagine the noisy, cheerful gatherings that took place at the Carline family's home at 47 Downshire Hill, not far from Pond Street, and I am glad that at last someone has recorded the vital contribution the Carline family made to Hampstead's artistic life between the wars. For too long, Hilda Carline and her family have remained relatively uncelebrated. This exhibition will do much to make them better known.

FRANCES SPALDING

Self-portrait
1913 (cat.5)
Water-colour, 300 × 210mm
Private collection

All works of art are by Hilda Carline unless stated otherwise

THE ART OF HILDA CARLINE

Mrs Stanley Spencer

'the most perfect, the happiest, most vital productive and serene time of all the years I have known'[1]

THUS Hilda Carline remembered her student days in London just before the outbreak of the First World War. Her statement reflects the enjoyment and sense of fulfilment from the two years spent at Percyval Tudor-Hart's School of Painting in Hampstead, London. These years represented the realisation of Hilda's long cherished ambition: to be allowed an opportunity to study art in London or Paris. Hilda knew that she was as talented and able as her artist brothers Sydney and Richard, but over the previous decade she had grown increasingly frustrated at being forced to remain quietly at home in Oxford while Sydney, older by one year, attended the Slade School of Fine Art, London. Then Richard, younger than Hilda by seven years, was permitted to join Sydney in Paris where the latter had gone after completing his studies at the Slade, eagerly seeking the new and experimental in painting. The year was 1912 and Sydney quickly discovered Cézanne, Gauguin, Van Gogh – and, living in Paris at that time, Percyval Tudor-Hart, a painter-teacher of eccentric personality with advanced ideas in painting and a set of aesthetic theories about colour and the laws which govern the visual emotions. Sydney became an enthusiastic disciple and successfully persuaded his father that his brother Richard should begin his artistic training at Tudor-Hart's Académie de Peinture in the Rue d'Assas. When Tudor-Hart transferred his school to Hampstead in the autumn of 1913, Sydney and Richard followed. To Hilda's great joy her father agreed that she could join her brothers in London: 'we were to take a few rooms or half a house & I was to keep house for the three of us, and thus be able at the same time to attend the school'.[2] With such an opportunity, Hilda's despondency at her lack-lustre life in Oxford quickly disappeared. She found Tudor-Hart's ideas refreshing and invigorating and the two years that Hilda spent at this school were critical for her development as an artist, as she herself later recognised: 'It is the period that has set its mark on all other events & thoughts, & that is ineffaceable, clear and pure.'[3]

When Hilda joined her two brothers in London, in the autumn of 1913, she was twenty-four years of age. Born in 1889, she was the fourth of five children. George (born 1886), Roland (born 1887), and Sydney (born 1888) were her elders and only Richard younger (born 1896). Hilda's father, also George, came from a family with a long history of involvement in the visual arts. His forebears comprised a succession of architect-builders, sculptors and painters, long centred in Shrewsbury. Indeed their craft pedigree could be traced back to the beginning of the eighteenth century. Hilda's

left to right:

George Carline in his Fulham Road studio, *c.*1892. On the lower right is George Carline's painting of Hilda, aged two, *All among the roses*

Annie Carline reading to her children, *c.*1892. From left to right: Annie, Hilda, Roland, Sydney and George

Hilda, *c.*1902

father, however, came from a Lincoln branch of the family. George Carline's own father had been a solicitor, serving twice as mayor of the city. He had decided early on that his youngest son George, born in 1855, would follow in the family tradition and train as an architect, but he did not live long enough to oversee his plan's fulfilment. George Carline was left free to follow his own inclinations towards a career as a painter and studied first at Heatherley's Art School, London, then in Antwerp and finally at the Académie Julian, Paris. He then returned to London, set up a studio on the Fulham Road and began to earn a living in the manner typical of professional artists of his time, taking on portrait, landscape, illustration and occasional advertising commissions, as well as regularly exhibiting subject pictures at the Royal Academy. In 1886 George Carline had his first work, *Spelling out the List*, accepted and hung on the line at the Royal Academy. It then went on a highly successful tour of galleries around the country over the next five years – a useful recommendation for ensuring a steady flow of work to support his rapidly expanding family. A year after his return to England George Carline married, and a mere four years later was father to three sons and a daughter.

The bare fact of George's marriage conceals a romantic story. While carrying out a portrait commission in Essex in 1885, he had fallen in love with and married his sitter's maid, Annie Smith. Annie's background was suitably mysterious: she was an orphan who had been brought up in Essex but retained vague childhood memories of visiting a grandmother living in Romany style on the Welsh Borders. As it happened, Annie Carline also possessed considerable artistic talent, but this had no opportunity for expression until middle age. After her husband's death in 1920 Annie Carline began writing children's stories, some of which were published. Wanting to illustrate her stories she began painting water-colours from nature – and rapidly developed her own distinctive, if naïve, style. Among the many admirers of her work were the French painters Chaim Soutine and André Lhote, and as the result of Lhote's support, Annie exhibited her work at the Galerie Pittoresque, Paris in 1939. Annie Carline could boast of being the only member of her family to have a show in Paris.

With such an inheritance it is hardly surprising that three of George and Annie Carline's children: Sydney, Richard and Hilda should become gifted artists. Of their other two children, George became an anthropologist while Roland died tragically of tuberculosis in 1906 at the early age of nineteen. Most of the Carline children's childhood was spent in Oxford. Their home was The Shrubbery, a large, well-proportioned house in tree-lined North Oxford with, as the name suggests, a garden full of yet more shrubs and trees. Throughout her career, trees were to figure prominently in Hilda's work: paintings of gardens full of spring blossom or trees in late autumn dripping with moisture and the last few unshed leaves, or drawings emphasizing the severe architectural forms of the bare-branched winter trees. Perhaps it was this childhood spent in a virtual arboretum which engendered her great sensitivity to their beauty of form and shifting subtlety of colour.

At The Shrubbery the young Carlines were surrounded by 'Da's' paintings: delicate genre pictures such as *An apron full of meadow flowers*, a portrait of Hilda aged two enchantingly plucking rose petals out of a straw hat, or another of her aged fifteen dressed as a red admiral butterfly for a children's fancy dress party. Relying on charm, as these pictures do for their appeal, they were nevertheless underpinned by a mastery of technical skills. George sought to pass on these skills to those three of his children who from an early age displayed a great aptitude for drawing and painting, which bordered on precociousness. A water-colour of a swan against a dark hedge painted by Richard at the age of three years and eleven months won him a Royal Drawing Society prize. Throughout her school career, Hilda also won many prizes for her drawing. In 1907 the Royal Drawing Society awarded her a special Certificate of Honour for the rare achievement of gaining Honours in all six divisions of the Society's examinations: Freehand, Elementary Perspective I and II, Growing Plants, Light and Shade and Painting from Casts. This was not Hilda's only achievement. The following year she left Oxford High School with a Higher School Certificate in French (special mention), Maths, History and Biology.

This summer of 1908 found Hilda in her nineteenth year, a highly intelligent,

left to right:

GEORGE CARLINE
Red admiral
1904 (cat.63)
Water-colour, 297 × 215mm
Private collection

Hilda and her brothers drawing, *c.*1896.
From left to right: Roland, Sydney, George and Hilda

SYDNEY CARLINE
Portrait of Hilda
*c.*1913 (cat.64)
Pencil on paper, 362 × 285mm
Private collection

Canal bridge
*c.*1909 (cat.3)
Water-colour, 290 × 224mm
Private collection

deep-thinking young woman who was, nevertheless, unsure of her way forward. She would dearly have loved to accompany her brother Sydney to the Slade School of Fine Art in London but there was little hope of this, given her father's initial lack of support to even Sydney studying art. This seeming change of attitude from his earlier supportive one may have been the result of the fact that around 1899, George Carline had lost much of his money in an unsuccessful business venture. Aware of the precarious nature of an artistic existence he may well have felt that his son would be better advised to pursue some other career. However, Sydney was so determined to become a painter that he earned the Slade fees for himself by producing and selling prints and making portrait medallions (over the years Sydney was to become well known for his portrait medals). Hilda, too, in her own way was equally determined. As was the fate of many young middle-class women in late Edwardian England, she was trapped in a trivial round of entertaining and visiting family and friends, and, being the only daughter, there was no one else who could fulfil her mother's desire for a companion and helper in domestic duties. However, whenever possible Hilda would escape to her father's studio to join him in painting the models that he regularly hired. Alternatively she might wander out of Oxford along the river Isis or canal towpath or into the meadows where she would paint the barges slowly drifting down the canal or sketch the cows knee-deep in summer buttercups. The result of these excursions is a rich and technically assured collection of early landscapes, portraits and figure work – subjects which were to continue to engage Hilda's interest throughout her life.

Understandably, the strongest influence on Hilda's work at this time stems from her father. Her early landscapes and portraits are quintessentially Victorian in their tightly controlled realism and choice of often charming and picturesque subject matter, as *Flower seller* (cat.1) demonstrates; other figures in the same vein include *The blind organ grinder*, or *The seamstress*. The best of these paintings possess a directness which stops them becoming merely decorative, such as the finely modelled *Head of an old man* (cat.2), which is a good example of Hilda's emerging talent as a portraitist. There is an empathy with the sitter. The old man seems more than a 'mere' model; there is a recognition of his dignity under the predicament of old age. The series of water-colours produced by Hilda between 1909 and 1912 are a great tribute to her commitment and ambition, but ultimately working in a state of semi-isolation in Oxford could not sustain her. Hilda found herself slipping into a state of depression in which even her own painting no longer held any interest for her: 'I was unhappy and seemed to have lost my ideals and ambitions'.[4] Thus, perhaps because of her depressive state, when the opportunity finally arose for Hilda to go to art school she was initially uninterested and unresponsive, leaving it to Sydney and her mother to make the necessary arrangements for her attendance. '[I] did not particularly mind what I did or where I went',[5] Hilda later wrote. This was in the autumn of 1913 when Sydney and Richard decided to follow Tudor-Hart from Paris to London.

Flower seller
1909–10 (cat.1)
Water-colour, 381 × 271mm
Private collection

Fortunately, this state of affairs did not last. Hilda's ambivalence vanished with the stimulation of 'the first hour of being in London'. She found just being in London and

Head of an old man
1909–10 (cat.2)
Water-colour, 392 × 285mm
Private collection

Bathing hut, Lincoln
1914 (cat.6)
Water-colour, 191 × 275mm
Private collection

walking the streets a 'revelation ... It seemed as unlike anything I had seen before as India might have been'.[6] Hilda also took great pride and pleasure in creating a home together with Sydney and Richard in the top half of 4 Downshire Hill, Hampstead. It did not matter that initially their sole furnishings consisted of garden and deck chairs as armchairs, or that they slept on camp-beds and used orange boxes as wash stands and dressing tables. All three were intensely proud of their new home and always showed visitors over the house who, as Hilda subsequently came to realize, could see 'none of the beauty that we felt to be there'.[7]

London was also an exciting place artistically in the years immediately prior to the outbreak of the First World War. The new ideas and developments in painting that Sydney and Richard had experienced in Paris were also making their mark in London, emanating from the series of controversial modern art exhibitions inaugurated most famously by Roger Fry's *Manet and the Post-Impressionists* exhibition at the Grafton Gallery in 1910. Other shows followed and Sydney's excitement at his own discovery of modern painting in Paris would undoubtedly have ensured that Hilda too would have shared in what was new and avant-garde in London. Likewise, his enthusiasm for Percyval Tudor-Hart's theories also ensured that Hilda attended an art school where students were encouraged to put these new ideas into practice. Tudor-Hart's teachings challenged every aspect of the creative process – relationships of colour, form, tone, even the subject-matter itself. This teaching had an immediate impact on Hilda's work. For example, the simplified forms and strongly articulated design of *Bathing hut, Lincoln* (cat.6), painted just months after joining Tudor-Hart's School, contrasts sharply with the detailed and carefully worked landscapes painted around Oxford. In *Bathing hut, Lincoln* Hilda has applied the paint in broad single colour washes and daringly enlivened the essentially tonal watercolour by a row of bright orange squares – representing the windows in the bathing hut. This watercolour also reflects some of Tudor-Hart's teachings on colour. An admirer of Kandinsky, Tudor-Hart devised a system of colour harmony analogous to that in music. He suggested that an artist, like a musical composer, paint a picture in a certain 'key' and change 'key' for specific visual or emotional effects. To help the artist in his choice of key, Tudor-Hart produced a series of complicated colour and tonal charts,[8] according to which the 'brightness and cheerfulness' of orange could be seen to aptly represent Hilda's mood at this time.

Despite Tudor-Hart's advanced ideas, he ran his school on traditional lines. Life-drawing classes, for example, were an important part of the curriculum *but* the drawings had to be produced in accordance with his 'three tone system of drawing'. The searching out and delineating of boundaries between the different tone values is evident in, for example, Hilda's drawing of the *Standing male nude* (cat.14) and translated into paint in her standing figure of *Man in grey* (cat.13). In composition classes Tudor-Hart still asked his students to tackle biblical and classical subjects – 'The Raising of Lazarus' or 'Ulysses Slaying the Pretenders' – but on other occasions he set abstract themes. Among Hilda's sketchbooks from this period are responses to 'Ode

left to right:

Still life with gold mirror and Buddha
1914 (cat.8)
Water-colour, 253 × 175mm
Private collection

Zeppelin over London
1915 (cat.9)
Oil on canvas, 225 × 225mm
Private collection

Man in grey
1915 (cat.13)
Oil on canvas, 574 × 440mm
Private collection

to a Dead Violet' by Shelley, the rhythm of Paul Verlaine's poem 'Les sanglots longs des violons' and instructions to express 'Joy in three colours, two tones and subdivisions'. From such exercises spring paintings such as *Still life with gold mirror and Buddha* (cat.8), *A Fantasy* (cat.7) and *Zeppelin over London* (cat.9) in which Hilda demonstrates a new expressive use of colour: the intense grey-cool calmness of the Buddha still-life or the menacing mood of the *Zeppelin over London* with its huge ball of blazing light hanging low in the dark night sky. The mood of impending disaster is heightened by the thick strokes of paint, possibly applied with a palette knife.

Hilda's two years at Tudor-Hart's School were an important period of stylistic experimentation evident, perhaps, in the small scale of much of the work that she produced at this time. Most importantly, it launched Hilda into the tide of twentieth-century painting. When Hilda joined Sydney and Richard in London she already was a technically skilled draughtswoman and water-colourist and so was, in a sense, 'free' to become involved with more aesthetic considerations. There is no doubt that Tudor-Hart's ideas made a deep impression on all three Carlines. Back in their shared flat, Hilda, Sydney and Richard and their friends endlessly debated their guru's ideas, and worked on their own paintings together, applying Tudor-Hart's critical criteria to their efforts. Not surprisingly their work has much in common both with regard to technique and subject-matter. The work of all three artists at this period is characterized by strong, broad planes of colours applied in a rich, painterly manner, simplified forms and a careful avoidance of the picturesque – most vehemently so by Richard. In paintings such as *A Fantasy* (cat.7) and *Return from the farm* (cat.17) Hilda conjures up a dreamlike sensibility. Similarly many of Sydney's works possess a quiet lyricism, for example, *The perambulator* (1913). Richard's work from about 1915 to 1920, by contrast, is marked by an unrelenting realism. He paints a particularly stark *Crucifixion* (1914) and a series of dour, matter-of-fact still-lifes, favouring inconsequential groupings of beer-bottles, dessicated-looking fruits and preferring faded to fresh flowers. When Richard paints his sister's portrait (cat.65) he makes no concessions to the severe cold

Hilda in an amateur dramatics production, *c.*1914

RICHARD CARLINE
Portrait of Hilda Carline
1918 (cat.65)
Oil on canvas, 762 × 635mm
Tate Gallery, London:
presented by the artist in 1976

from which she was suffering, and faithfully records her red nose: part of the 'objective truth' to which he aimed. Always fearful of flattery, he has still produced a sensitive and perceptive portrait of his sister that pays heed to her serious and thoughtful nature.

Richard Carline's portrait of Hilda was painted in April 1918 during a brief break in his service with the Royal Flying Corps where his duties included painting aerial views of the Western Front for training purposes. The outbreak of the First World War had split up the Carlines' close group. Both Sydney and Richard joined the Royal Flying Corps; Sydney first, in 1915, and Richard after a period in an experimental camouflage unit – run by none other than Tudor-Hart himself! In 1916 Hilda together with Cora Stoop, a friend and fellow student at Tudor-Hart's School, joined the Land Army. Hilda and Cora worked together on a farm near Wangford, Suffolk, doing general farm work. There are photographs of the friends dressed in the Government issue gaitered work shoes and heavy corduroy skirts working in the fields – ploughing and helping with the harvest. They worked from ten to twelve hours a day, six days a week, but when off-duty they lived a quasi-Bohemian existence in a richly carved Romany caravan parked on the farmer's land. It was hard work, but also a happy and fulfilling period. For many artists, the war years brought about a suspension of normal activity, but perhaps in Hilda's case this could be seen as having a positive result. The fallow period allowed Hilda, albeit unconsciously, to distil out of Tudor-Hart's teachings those aspects that had the greatest meaning and relevance to her. The work she produced upon her return to London possesses great strength and integrity in which it is possible to recognise Hilda's fully realised mature style.

The demobilisation of 1919, with the return of the male work-force, meant that Hilda's services as a Land Girl were no longer needed. She returned to London, but it was to a very different life to the one she had enjoyed with Sydney and Richard in their flat before the war. In 1916 George and Annie Carline had left Oxford to establish a new family home only a few doors away from their children's former studios, in 'one of the two semi-detached Georgian family houses which held one another up at the corner of Keats Grove'. Hilda's new home at 47 Downshire Hill, Hampstead, was

Land Girls: Hilda and Cora Stoop
Suffolk, *c.*1917

The Romany caravan, *c.*1917. Hilda and her brother George enjoying afternoon tea outside the Romany caravan, where she and Cora lived as Land Girls

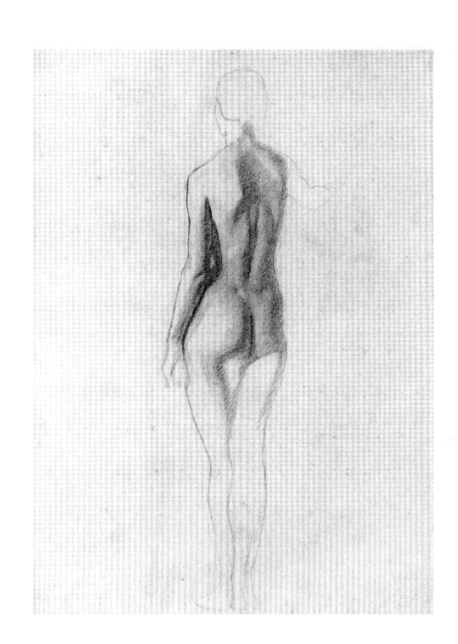

Back view of a female nude
1915 (cat.11)
Pencil on paper, 382 × 276mm
Private collection

a somewhat subdued one, with just Hilda and her parents in occupation. Sydney and Richard were still absent, now working as Official War Artists in the Middle East. Hilda consequently found it difficult to settle back down to life in London. She missed the camaraderie and shared sense of purpose that she had enjoyed with her brothers and fellow students at Tudor-Hart's School. Her friend Cora's energies were now being diverted in other directions as she had recently married and was pregnant. Hilda found herself confronting her mother's domestic expectations which she frankly found 'irksome'. A reason to escape from the house was urgently needed, which she found by enrolling as a part-time student at the Slade School of Fine Art, London.

The Slade's teaching methods were the complete antithesis to those of Tudor-Hart. The emphasis at the Slade was on drawing rather than painting and there was minimal instruction on colour. Furthermore, the Slade Professor, Henry Tonks, had little time for Post-Impressionism or any of the new non-representational movements in art. He insisted that his students spent long days drawing and eventually painting the life model and encouraged his students to draw and paint naturalistically. The way into the Life Room was via success in the Antique Room – a studio full of casts of Classical and Renaissance sculpture – where the students had first to demonstrate their proficiency in drawing the sculptured human form. Even Hilda, who had considerable experience of life drawing and a portfolio of drawings to prove her competency, was granted no concessions and had to spend her first term in this 'museum'. She jumped this hurdle effortlessly, sharing first prize in the competition 'Painting the Cast' in June 1919. She went on to win other prizes for her figure-drawing and painting. Numerous fine drawings and a group of sumptuous oils show how richly deserved this recognition was. Front, back, side view, full length, a concentration on the torso or hips or legs or hands, Hilda explored the human body from seemingly every vantage. She obviously enjoyed these regular sessions at the Slade: her drawings are full of grace and vigour – and great technical virtuosity. The classes also served to sharpen the acuteness of her observational skills which were fully evident in later years in a series of keenly observed portraits such as her own *Self-portrait* (cat.39), *Woman in a red hat* (cat.29) and *Elsie* (cat.43). The Slade's emphasis on the human figure rekindled Hilda's interest in portraiture which had largely lain dormant under Tudor-Hart's focus on more abstract considerations.

In the Life Room, Hilda willingly submitted to the Slade's philosophy of carefully wrought naturalism but outside the Slade she maintained her own independent vision. *Bathing tents* (cat.18) with its high horizon, bold geometric shapes and rich glowing colours is one such work: quite unrelated to the carefully wrought tonal nudes Hilda painted at the Slade. *Cliffs, Seaford* (cat.19) is another striking seascape. From a vertiginous viewpoint atop the massive chalk cliffs of the Sussex coast Hilda looked directly and precipitously down onto the sand and sea below. Hilda might well have chosen the unusual and dramatic perspective of this seascape after looking at some of the landscapes that her brothers produced after their war experiences in the

Royal Flying Corps. They were probably the first artists in Britain to paint landscapes from the air, and noticeable in many of these aerial compositions is the complete lack of reference to any sky-line and a preoccupation with surface pattern. A similar strong design, together with Gauguinesque broad planes of colour, can also be seen in another significant work – *Return from the farm* (cat.17). But that is where the the similarity between the two works ends. Hilda painted Cora Stoop and herself leisurely returning from the farm on their favourite horse after a day's war service in the fields. A sense of tranquillity is ably evoked by this summer-evening landscape. Hilda entered this painting for the Slade's Figure Composition Competition in 1919 without success. While the Symbolist quality of the picture with its lack of emphasis on the figures would not have won Tonks's approval, *Return from the farm* would certainly have found admirers among a group of friends who gathered around Hilda, Sydney and Richard Carline in the 1920s.

In the autumn of 1919, Sydney and Richard Carline finished their war work in the Middle East and joined Hilda and their parents at 47 Downshire Hill. They also rented two large studios in the former Church School opposite, where Hilda became 'The Passage Artist' having only the long side passage in which to work. These studios at 14A Downshire Hill and the family home across the road became a focal point for Hampstead's artistic and intellectual life during the 1920s. Henry Lamb, James (Jas) Wood, Richard Hartley and Stanley and Gilbert Spencer, as well as Mark Gertler, John and Paul Nash, Boris von Anrep, Christopher Nevinson, Charles Ginner, William Roberts, Kathleen Hale, Dorothy Brett and Ethelbert White were frequent visitors to the Carline studios where they would draw the models the Carlines hired or even draw and paint each other. After a day's work these artist-friends would retire for supper at the Carline family home where still others might join them. Often ten or even occasionally twenty visitors would sit around the log fire and enjoy debates which often extended late into the night: 'there was considerable reliance placed on Jas Wood to stimulate the discussion, which might otherwise hang fire until his taxi was heard drawing up outside. Stanley or Henry would soon be provoked into the debate relieved by the humourous actions and interjections of Richard Hartley'.[9] Hilda, by temperament, was not as outgoing as many members of this group but Gilbert Spencer once observed that 'when she talked she was always interesting'.[10]

There is some evidence that the group of friends tried to adopt a conscious group identity. Henry Lamb referred to their group as the '*cercle pan-artistique* of Downshire Hill' and praised its 'corrective stimulus' to the RA Schools in letters to Richard Carline, and discussed whether they should admit Edwin John (son of Augustus) to its 'membership'. Certainly the *cercle* could be seen as encompassing many of the more advanced trends of inter-war English painting with most of its members exhibiting with the London Group, a showcase of modernity in the early 1920s. Founded in 1913, this exhibiting forum owed its origin to a sense of frustration with existing institutions such as the Royal Academy and the New English Art Club at their failure to accept the new ideas of Post-Impressionism, Fauvism, Cubism and Futurism. The

London Group was always careful to avoid associating itself specifically with any of these new movements but provided a forum where anyone could exhibit freely and without aesthetic constraint. In the immediate post-war years, its regular showings at Heals were eagerly awaited and widely reported. Throughout the early 1920s Hilda usually had a painting in a London Group exhibition, yet she never sought official membership as Sydney and Richard did.

Undoubtedly the return to England of Hilda's brothers, her regular drawing sessions at the Slade, her associations with the *cercle pan-artistique* and the London Group gave Hilda new confidence. Consequently, the early 1920s were some of her most artistically productive years. It was also the time of her developing relationship with Stanley Spencer. Hilda and Stanley met in December 1919 at a Carline family dinner. The First World War had interrupted a developing friendship between Hilda's brother Richard and Stanley Spencer. They did not meet again until December 1919 at a huge show of war paintings held at the Royal Academy, at which they both exhibited. Richard invited Stanley to supper, a meal he recalled with great clarity many years afterwards. There was soup as the starter which Hilda had served. 'As Hilda came round to me', wrote Stanley in 1942, 'I thought how extra-ordinary she looked. I felt sure she had the same mental attitude towards things as I had. I could feel my true self in that extra-ordinary person. I saw life with her'.[11] Although this first meeting undoubtedly assumed a heightened significance over the years, there is no mistaking the strong impression that Hilda had made on Stanley that December evening, and he was intrigued by Hilda, not only as a woman but also as a painter. Although virtually penniless, he wrote to her a couple of weeks later asking if he could buy for three guineas a little painting of a group of sheep that Hilda had shown him that memorable evening.[12] He felt 'there is something heavenly in it' and 'the more I look at it, the more I love it'.[13] Stanley was to maintain a deep admiration for Hilda's work throughout his life.

However strong his feelings might have been towards Hilda, Stanley had to be content for the time being to confine his admiration to Hilda's paintings alone. Stanley had a rival for Hilda's affections in his own brother Gilbert. Younger than Stanley by a year, Gilbert had returned to the Slade in 1919 to complete his studies which had been interrupted by the war, where he had met Hilda. 'No ordinary girl', he later wrote, 'she always seemed to be thinking very hard about something, though this did not inhibit her enchanting sense of humour and fun' and 'with her auburn hair – she bore some resemblance to Whistler's *Symphony in White* – was a sight to stir anyone romantically inclined'.[14] Indeed Gilbert and Stanley were not the only ones to be 'romantically stirred'; another member of the *cercle pan-artistique*, Jas Wood, had been in love with Hilda but she had decided a long-term relationship between them could not endure. Unexpectedly she was compelled to decide between Gilbert and Stanley. Stanley had accepted Gilbert's prior claim on Hilda's affections for six months, but then the brothers, always good friends, decided the rivalry had to be resolved. One summer's day in 1920 Gilbert escorted Hilda to their home in Cookham, Berkshire and she was boldly asked to state her preference! She chose Stanley.

When Hilda and Stanley first met in 1919 she was already thirty and Stanley twenty-eight. Hilda had enjoyed a less parochial upbringing than Stanley, having lived in both London and Oxford as well as travelling widely in England and abroad. Stanley's childhood had been exclusively spent in the Thames-side village of Cookham to which he maintained an intense and mystical lifetime attachment. His was a self-contained childhood. His education had been largely undertaken by his two elder sisters Annie and Florence. Stanley's childhood haunts were the meadows and reedy river banks around the Thames at Cookham. These, together with the church and its churchyard, formed the setting for many of his well-known biblical and figure paintings as well as providing the subject-matter for his more straightforward landscapes. In contrast to the strong focus on the visual arts throughout Hilda's childhood, the dominant influence in the Spencer household had been music. 'Pa', William Spencer, was a local organist and teacher of music. Stanley's two eldest brothers, Will and Harold, progressed from child prodigies to professional pianist and violinist respectively. His other three elder brothers and two elder sisters played instruments so that Stanley, youngest but one in this large family of nine children, was brought up surrounded by the constant playing and appreciation of music. Stanley always enjoyed music but, nevertheless, he and his younger brother Gilbert chose art for their careers. Initially surprised by their choice, their father did not hinder them but sought out the best for his sons. In 1908 Stanley led the way to the Slade School, where he was a contemporary of Hilda's brother Sydney. Though the two shared a Slade summer prize in 1909, Stanley and Sydney seemed to have had no more than a passing acquaintance as students. Indeed Stanley's limited experience and confined upbringing kept him at an intellectual and social distance from most of the other students with their public school backgrounds and well-to-do homes. Stanley travelled up each day from Cookham and spent his days working hard in the Life Room. Just as Hilda was to experience a decade later, the Slade's great emphasis was on drawing, which came to assume a central role in Stanley's work. After his four years at the Slade, Stanley returned to living full-time in Cookham and began the transformation of his keenly-felt everyday experiences into works of monumental and visionary significance. Before the war, these key experiences were 'the Slade with life drawing ... the life at home, and the feeling the Bible gave me'[15] which prompted such characteristic works as *Zacharias and Elizabeth* (1914), *The centurion's servant* (1914) and *Mending cowls, Cookham* (1915).[16]

The outbreak of war in 1914 interrupted Stanley's flow of work as the general patriotic fervour overtook him. His mother, worried about his small stature, persuaded Stanley to opt for ambulance work. After a spell as a medical orderly at Beaufort War Hospital near Bristol, he volunteered for service overseas and was assigned to the 68th Field Ambulances in Macedonia and for the last few months of the war, he fought as an infantryman with the 7th Battalion of the Berkshire Regiment. In December 1918, Stanley was on leave in Cookham pending demobilisation. After his profound experiences of the Front, it was unrealistic to expect him to simply pick up the threads of his old life and recapture the same 'vision'. For the first time in his life, Stanley felt restless and impatient. Such post-war disorientation was, of course, not unique. As was true for many artists who survived the war, Stanley found expression for his pent-up feelings by painting works inspired by his wartime experience. He started painting *Travoys arriving with wounded at a dressing station, Smol, Macedonia 1916*.[17] Stanley could have emphasized the terrible sufferings of the wounded men but instead, as he later explained to Hilda, 'standing a little away from the old Greek church, which we used as a dressing station and operating theatre ... I felt there was a grandeur [to the scene] ... a spiritual ascendency over everything'.[18] From Stanley's war paintings emanates a tremendous feeling of calm and even a sense of quiet, ordered acceptance of events. This presentation of scenes of war must have come as a surprising contrast at the large exhibition of war paintings at the Royal Academy in December 1919, where inevitably most scenes of the war concentrated on the horror and brutality.

From an early stage in their relationship, Stanley had intented to marry Hilda, but there were pressing practical considerations which made such a scheme difficult. Stanley was not in a financial position to support a wife and possible family. During the early 1920s Stanley was leading a particularly precarious peripatetic existence. Sometimes prompted by the promise of commissions – which typically did not always 'work out' – at other times glad to accept a friend's hospitality, he moved between Bourne End, Reading, Steep and Petersfield (both in Hampshire) and Durweston and Poole in Dorset. Whenever possible he visited London, wanting to maintain his contacts with the *cercle pan-artistique* and, of course, to see Hilda. Happily, in the summer of 1922 the opportunity arose for Hilda and Stanley to spend several months together. The Carlines (Hilda, her mother, brothers George, Sydney and Richard and cousin May Pigott) invited Stanley to join them on a summer painting expedition to Bosnia. Although Stanley had no enthusiasm for foreign travel, the desire to be with Hilda prompted him to accept their invitation. It was indeed a major undertaking. The party travelled across Europe, stopping en route for five days in Vienna, where they used the opportunity to visit art galleries. Once in Bosnia they visited Sarajevo, Mostar, Ragusa (Dubrovnik), Montenegro, Padorizza and Lake Scutari. They then returned to Ragusa, before journeying on to Split where they embarked on a ship to Trieste. They made the return journey to England overland via Munich and Cologne.

Hilda was an experienced and original landscape painter who greatly enjoyed the opportunities that such family excursions gave her to explore different types of scenery. Stanley was less enthusiastic about landscape, hitherto tending to view the painting of landscape as a 'lifeless mechanical chore' only relevant as a backcloth to his imaginative figure paintings. However, working with his brother Gilbert at Durweston in Dorset in 1920 he had begun to change his ideas (and he was beginning to realize the freedom to be gained by the emerging commercial value of his landscapes!).

STANLEY SPENCER
Sarajevo
1922 (cat.67)
Oil on canvas, 360 × 253mm
South London Art Gallery

Waterfall, Mostar
1922 (cat.36)
Oil on canvas, 554 × 445mm
Private collection

View of Mostar
1922. The location of this painting is unknown

Sitting beside Hilda on the hillside above Mostar and in the olive groves of Ragusa, his conversion to enthusiasm for the genre was complete. Stanley's Bosnian landscapes are among the boldest and most original that he ever painted. None of Stanley's landscapes, though, can quite compete with Hilda's painting of *Waterfall, Mostar* (cat.36) for its utilization of clean forms and strongly articulated design. This work can be seen as belonging to Hilda's series of uncompromising landscapes begun in Tudor-Hart days and which includes such works as *Bathing tents* (cat.18) and *Cliffs, Seaford* (cat.19). In *Waterfall, Mostar,* Hilda employed again, as she did two years previously in her painting of *Lake Orta,* at Brolo (cat.24), gentle saturated tones – soft pinky beige, buffs, olive green. Such tones can also be seen in Stanley's painting *River Nareta, Mostar.*[19] Hilda also painted a view of the River Nareta. The location of the painting is presently unknown but, with its elevated viewpoint looking out over the River Nareta to the towns and hills beyond, it is a particularly fine landscape. Hilda and Stanley also made several oil and water-colour paintings of the mosques of Sarajevo, obviously both attracted by the soaring vertical wooden minarets which slice across the horizontal divisions of the landscapes.

Both Hilda and Stanley appear to have been conscious of a new closeness which emerged from this first prolonged opportunity to spend time together. 'In the train going to Sarajevo, Hilda and I slept alongside each other fully dressed, head to feet. Hilda was wearing a grey dress and a coat with grey braid ... In Sarajevo we only got as far as Hilda taking my arm, but *that* I can remember – the first direct and deliberate expression of liking for me.'[20] On the back of one of Hilda's Sarajevo water-colours are scribbled the words: 'Done on the occasion of Stanley first proposing to me', which seems to be confirmation of the encouragement this gesture gave Stanley. Hilda and Stanley returned to England engaged, but a few months later Stanley unexpectedly broke it off. It would seem that he was panicked by catching a glimpse of Hilda standing on a table being measured for her wedding dress. A few months later, equally

capriciously, Stanley renewed their engagement. This sequence of breaking and renewing their engagement occurred 'six or seven times' according to Hilda. Her family and friends grew increasingly perplexed and annoyed with Stanley. Hilda seems to have been remarkably unperturbed by Stanley's indecisiveness. It was as if Hilda understood that this on and off nature of their engagement was a necessary part of their developing relationship. At the time, they both believed in the sacred and indissoluble nature of marriage and needed to be convinced of the rightness of their bond. Both were subject to intense feelings and would endlessly analyse and define their thoughts and emotions. Neither would willingly concede defeat in argument. They would walk together on Hampstead Heath thrashing out their ideas, endlessly exchanging their views on Art and Religion. From the outset Hilda and Stanley expressed their differences with candour, even bluntness, which perhaps ultimately was unhelpful to both of them and caused irrevocable damage to their relationship. This frankness is evident even in their pre-nuptial letters: the beginnings of a vast and infinitely various correspondence which continued throughout their lives, and one-sidedly even after Hilda's death. The letters that Stanley wrote Hilda from Poole in 1923[21] were by turn dismissively critical and tenderly loving. Annoyed that Hilda liked a still-life of a hyacinth which he considered 'absolutely devoid of any idea of mine', Stanley bluntly told Hilda, 'It is rather comical that I hate myself & love my ideas, whereas with you I hate your ideas and love you'.[22] Hilda would no doubt have felt relieved to receive the subsequent letter in which he assures her that 'you are the most secret & greatest joy of my life, you are like redemption to me. I think of you all the time ... I now know if I have you I shall find my life is full'.[23]

Despite the bewilderment of the Carlines at his seemingly inconsistent intentions towards Hilda, Stanley gradually became accepted as part of Hilda's family. Early in 1923, and again at the end of the year, Stanley lived with the Carlines and greatly prized the opportunity for close proximity to Hilda: 'I used to love passing the open door of her bedroom and see her changing some stockings, and just for a moment her pearly leg, and she loved to show as much leg as possible'.[24] At the beginning of 1924 Stanley obtained a permanent base in London. Henry Lamb decided to settle in Poole and sublet his studio in the Vale of Health Hotel, Hampstead to Stanley. Hilda and Stanley thus continued to be in daily contact and Stanley frequently came to supper at Downshire Hill. The three friends would often work together. Hilda painted Stanley; Stanley painted Richard; Richard painted Hilda and Stanley while Hilda painted herself, resulting in a fascinating set of portraits which reveal much about their various relationships and interchange of ideas. Richard Carline's painting is the most ambitious. Hilda and Stanley are featured as part of a large group portrait *Gathering on the terrace* (cat.66) which Richard painted in 1925. It is an interesting work in which he has carefully organized his figures within the space of the canvas so as to paint eight separate portraits of his family and close friends, whilst avoiding defining the relationships between them. Hilda and Stanley stand either side of the open doorway, gazes averted from each other, each engrossed in their own thoughts. Be-

RICHARD CARLINE
Gathering on the terrace
1925 (cat.66)
Oil on canvas, 1950 × 1613mm
Ferens Art Gallery, Kingston upon Hull

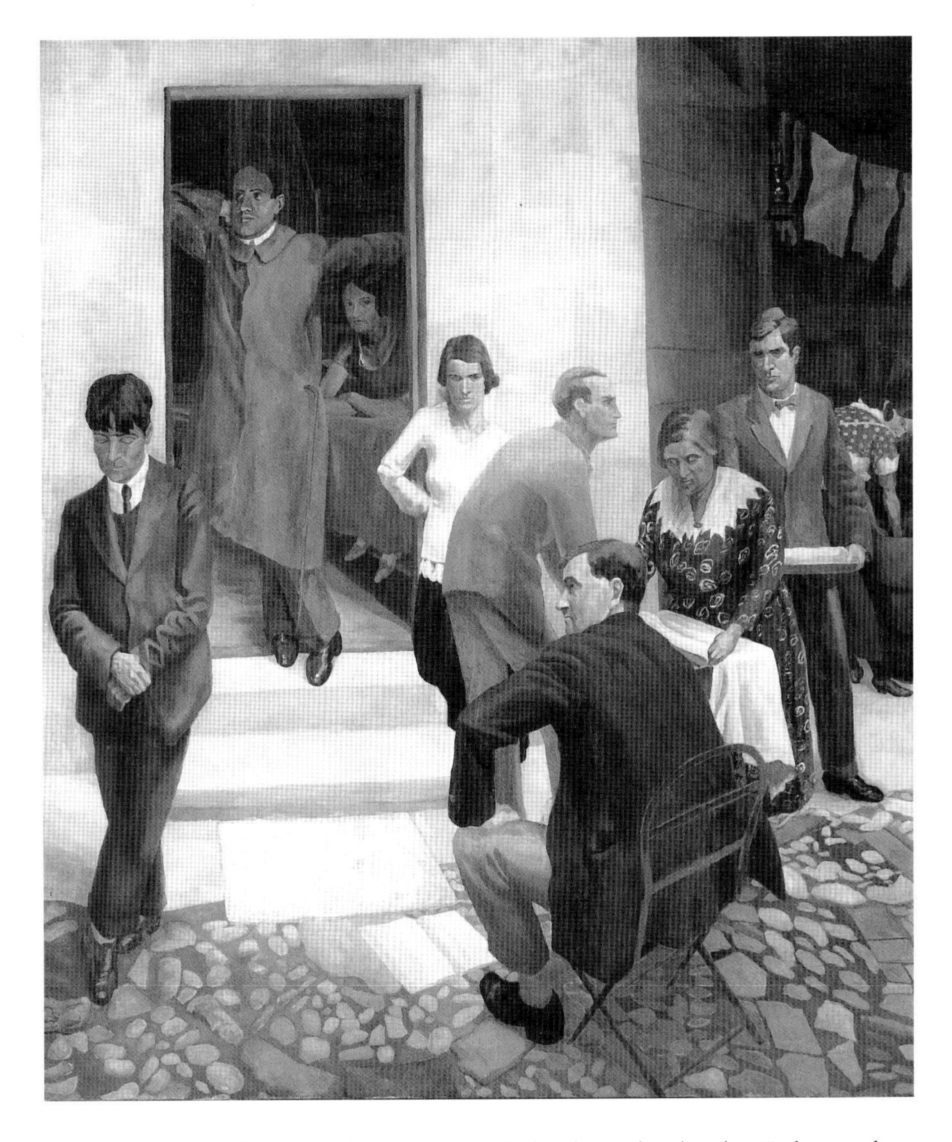

sides his sister and future brother-in-law are Richard's mother, brother Sydney and his friends Henry Lamb, Jas Wood, Richard Hartley and Kate Foster. This was the second large group portrait that Richard Carline painted. Two years previously he had painted Hilda, his brothers Sydney and George and his mother sitting, in self-contained silence, around their dining-room table at Downshire Hill. In this earlier group portrait he had included himself leaning against a cupboard.

The challenge of group portraiture, or conversation piece, attracted other members of the *cercle pan-artistique* during the 1920s. Henry Lamb painted pictures of the Anrep, Behrend, Japp and Kennedy families. In 1921 Hilda had painted a large group portrait of *Count Tossa's children* (cat.23). She met the Tossa family when the Carlines were on holiday in Northern Italy during the summer and autumn of 1920 when she made a series of pencil drawings of the children. Back in England, Hilda worked up her drawings into a major composition. As in her brother's conversation piece, one is immediately struck by the four children's air of detachment. They sit or stand atop a stone wall, gazes averted, each preoccupied with his or her own thoughts. The isolation of each child is disturbingly accentuated by their expressionless faces and wooden poses. Behind them is a richly painted bank of vegetation from which another, female, figure mysteriously emerges. Is she the children's mother? The dream-like, almost surreal, quality of this group portrait contrasts with the sharply focused intensity and direct confrontational gaze of the self-portrait that Hilda was to paint two years later.

Hilda had often drawn and occasionally painted herself in water-colour over the decade and a half preceding her 1923 self-portrait (cat.39), but never with such assurance as in this first essay in oils. Previously Hilda would sit or stand close to the mirror, anxiously confronting her own image with an analytical eye. In 1923, in the intimate space of her tiny personal sanctuary in Downshire Hill, Hilda has taken a few steps back from the mirror. As if posing for a formal portrait, yet with an unflinching gaze, Hilda dispassionately appraises herself. She sees a thoughtful young woman and she wants us to know that she is a serious working artist. Quietly in the bottom corner of the frame is Hilda's paintbox with its neat rows of brushes and tubes of paint. She has, it seems, put these brushes and paint to good use. The richly glowing colours, subtle composition and sensitively modelled face proclaim a skilled portraitist. Realising that sooner or later she would become Stanley's wife, it was perhaps important to Hilda to define her status as an artist by means of this strong statement of individual identity. She is considerably more diffident in her portrait of Stanley (cat.38) painted in the same year. Tentative in their newly formed relationship, artist and sitter do not confront each other directly. Stanley tilts his head to one side and averts his gaze away from Hilda leaving her free to explore the face of the man she loved. The result reveals a handsome young man with glossy black hair and sensuous lips. Stanley was obviously intrigued by Hilda's painting of himself, for when he painted a self-portrait in that same year he abandoned his usual confrontational full-face pose and instead half turns his head to quizzically study himself.[25] Oddly perhaps, Stanley did not attempt a reciprocal formal portrait of Hilda but includes her in a major new painting that he began in 1924 – *The Resurrection, Cookham*.[26] Stanley had long been attracted by the theme of Resurrection, and had already painted several Resurrection pictures. The 1924 version was by far the most ambitious. Through the imagery of the Resurrection Stanley celebrates his belief that heaven could be experienced on earth if only altruistic love could regulate human relations. The revelation of eternity is staged in his beloved Cookham churchyard. Rising from their graves, alongside the great Judeo-Christian prophets, are members of Stanley's family and close friends, with Hilda making no less than three appearances. She reclines on an ivy-covered tomb; she climbs over a stile on her way to the 'River of Life' and rises from another tomb smelling a flower. As Stanley later explained, she 'wonders about its scent and pushed it against her face. She wears a jumper I liked, one that had been pulled into being, very flopped from much washing of it'.[27] If Hilda needed reassurance of Stanley's feelings for her, here was full affirmation of them.

GILBERT SPENCER
Portrait of Hilda
1925 (cat.72)
Pencil on paper, 295 × 177mm
Private collection

Miss Silcox
1925 (cat.42)
Pencil drawing, 354 × 253mm
Private collection

On 23 February 1925, Hilda and Stanley's protracted courtship finally came to fruition; they married at Wangford Parish Church. Hilda's happy memories of her two war years spent as a Land Girl had prompted her wish to return to this Suffolk village for her marriage. It was a quiet wedding with Hilda's brothers Sydney and George and a family friend Miss Lilley as the only witnesses. Hilda's wedding outfit comprised a brown and black striped velvet suit 'with flapping sleeves' (which she had made herself) and a large tricorn hat which was to become another 'significant' memory for Stanley. Twenty years later Hilda appears in one of his Scrapbook Drawings dressed in this wedding outfit. Hilda and Stanley honeymooned locally at the Red Cottage and the bedroom in which they first shared their love was to become a place of pilgrimage for Stanley in years to come. After a week of honeymoon Stanley's brother, Gilbert, joined the couple, invited somewhat surprisingly by Hilda herself! Several years later in a letter to his wife, Stanley told her how he 'was absolutely astonished when 8 days after we married you asked Gil to come & stay'.[28] Perhaps Hilda suddenly felt nervous of spending a long time alone with Stanley's occasionally overwhelming personality.

The honeymoon became a painting holiday and took on the rhythm of former Carline holidays. The three artists painted during the day and read and discussed their work in the evenings. They also made portrait drawings of each other. Stanley's drawing of his new wife is full of obvious affection. Hilda sits writing with her head bowed and eyes slightly upturned. Her left hand is raised to her mouth with its symbol of their recent union prominently displayed on her wedding finger. Gilbert's drawing of his former love is a more formal effort. During their stay in Wangford Hilda, Stanley and Gilbert made several excursions to the nearby seaside town of Southwold where they drew and *tried* to paint Miss Silcox, the headmistress of Southwold Girls School who is believed to be a family friend of the Carlines. Whether this was as a commission or by way of a friendly favour, Hilda, Stanley and Gilbert decided to attempt her portrait. The results, however, were not very satisfactory. Stanley scraped out his and Hilda left her painting unfinished when Miss Silcox became tired of the protracted sittings, and Gilbert's effort is unrecorded. It is more than likely that Miss Silcox was a difficult sitter who found it impossible to relax. In Hilda's unfinished portrait Miss Silcox sits alert and rather tense in a high-backed red armchair with her hands tightly clasped. A similar tension is evident in a drawing that Hilda made of the headmistress (cat.42), presumably before starting the painting. The trio were happily more successful when, with the coming of the early spring, they were able to take their easels outside. Stanley painted *Trees and chicken coop, Wangford*,[29] Gilbert *The Windmill, Wangford* and Hilda, more ambitiously, a panoramic view of *Smoke from the Southwold train, Wangford* (cat.41). In choosing this unusual elongated format Hilda produced a marvellously expansive landscape in which 'space' is handled in a particularly interesting way. This wide-angle format produces a broad sweeping vista of the countryside while the lane cuts vertically across the picture to carry us into the far distance towards the concealed Southwold train.

Hilda and Shirin, *c.*1928

From Wangford, Hilda and Stanley returned to Hampstead to live together in the same Vale of Health studio where Stanley had been living before their marriage. Stanley resumed work on *The Resurrection, Cookham*. Hilda, however, could not re-establish her prenuptial involvement in her work. Although her honeymoon had been a productive time, back in London she found it impossible to work. Various factors probably contributed to this state of affairs, not least because Hilda and Stanley were living in cramped conditions. Presumably the newly-weds had one or two other rooms in the Vale of Health Hotel besides the studio, but this certainly was dominated by Stanley's immense *Resurrection* painting measuring some eighteen feet by nine! Furthermore, Hilda was pregnant and feeling ill much of the time. A daughter, Shirin, was born on 18 November 1925, and the unmistakable joy that Hilda experienced is expressed in a beautiful drawing that Hilda made of a bowl of paper-white narcissi just three days later. The fact remains, however, that in less than a year Hilda's life had dramatically changed. She was now married, she had a demanding baby and Stanley was proving to be not the easiest of people with whom to share one's life. In fact it took Hilda several years to readjust to these changes, and nearly four years were to elapse before Hilda did another major painting.

Hilda no doubt recognized and accepted the fact that their early years of marriage were critical ones for Stanley in terms of his professional career. He planned *The Resurrection, Cookham* to be the centrepiece of his first solo show at the Goupil Gallery, London, to open in February 1927. The exhibition caused a sensation. Opinion was fairly equally divided for and against the painting, but all the critics agreed that it was a remarkable work. Thereafter Stanley was to become a public figure and his reputation was very definitely established. *The Resurrection, Cookham* was bought by the Duveen Fund for £1000 and presented to the Tate Gallery. Whatever Hilda might have felt about her own difficulties she was always an enthusiastic supporter (and discerning critic) of her husband's work and she certainly never begrudged him his success.

The month of May 1927 brought a move out of London to Burghclere, a small village in the Hampshire countryside, five miles south of Newbury. This was to enable Stanley to work on a major commission, the decoration of the interior of a war memorial chapel. This was a project of enormous personal significance to Stanley which for the next five years set a totally different pattern to his and Hilda's life. For several years after the First World War Stanley had envisioned building a chapel, the walls of which he would cover with paintings reflecting his wartime experiences as an orderly in Beaufort Hospital, Bristol, and at the Macedonian Front. In fact he drew out a whole architectural scheme for a building, and was working on designs for his cycle of paintings at Henry Lamb's house in Poole in the summer of 1923 when Louis and Mary Behrend paid him a visit. The Behrends were so impressed by Stanley's ideas that they gave him the commission to create 'his' chapel as a memorial to Mary Behrend's brother, Lieutenant Henry Willoughby Sandham, who had died in 1919 from an illness contracted during his wartime service in Macedonia. They bought a

Stanley, Hilda and Shirin Burghclere, *c.*1928

site near their home at Burghclere and instructed their architect to construct the building exactly as Stanley had conceived it, to be known as the Sandham Chapel. In the spring of 1927 the chapel was ready, but not the cottage which the Behrends were also generously building for Hilda and Stanley. With his *Resurrection* painting finished Stanley was understandably eager to begin this grand project. Thus, in May 1927 Hilda, Stanley and eighteen-month-old Shirin moved to Burghclere and rented a room in nearby Palmer's Hill Farm.

Hilda understood the importance of this project for Stanley but her early spring visits with Stanley to view progress on the chapel had not endeared the village to her. Retrospectively she wrote, 'I knew of no place in England that seemed to me more meaningless than this, it seemed just like a blank on the map'. She was however more content at Palmer's Hill Farm than she had expected. Painting was still impossible. but it was difficult not to be won over by the good humour and kindness of the farmer Mr Forrester and his wife. Mrs Forrester cooked them wonderful meals and would often take charge of Shirin and amuse her, 'It was a great comfort to us to have the babe taken off our hands in this pleasant way at times'.[30] Hilda meanwhile found an outlet for her creative talents by designing the interior of their new cottage – even if the results were, by some accounts, not altogether practical! – and planning a garden. The results here were more successful and in the summers to come the garden became a mass of sweet-scented flowers. Drawing upon her wartime farming knowledge, Hilda was able to keep the family supplied with fresh fruit and vegetables and supply them to their visitors too. Hilda and Stanley loved to tell the tale of some departing friends who were presented with one of Hilda's cauliflowers wrapped in brown paper, which by chance had the Spencers' address on it. A few days later an anxious postman returned their parcel saying it had been found alongside the railway line!

Shortly after Christmas 1927, Chapel View Cottage was ready for habitation and on 10 February 1928, Hilda, Stanley and Shirin moved into their first proper home together. Two weeks later Elsie Munday, 'a local girl of sterling character', joined them to help with the housework and minding Shirin. Hilda eagerly looked forward to being able to resume her painting while Stanley worked on his epic cycle in the Sandham Chapel, but once again she found herself frustrated. 1928 was a year of developing tension and discord between Stanley and herself ending with Hilda feeling so 'hopeless and crushed' that she decided it was best for them to spend some time apart. Hilda had not entered into marriage with Stanley with any illusions as to their differences in character and temperament. She could not help but be aware of Stanley's forthright views and expectations, but she too had her own independent ideas which she was ready to defend. And yet it was this very difference in views which heightened an underlying clash of temperaments and clouded the deep love that they felt for each other. Seeds of future discord were evident even when Hilda and Stanley were living in the Vale of Health Hotel. There had been disagreements between Hilda and Stanley on household matters; Stanley believed that he knew best 'how to nurse the baby, wash the nappies and cook'. Hilda was not totally impractical in these matters, as Stanley often suggested, but he could not accept her different way of doing things. In Chapel View, Elsie's presence and help eased some of these tensions but created others in their place. Stanley liked to arrange his day into packets of organized activities and greatly admired Elsie's similar organizational qualities, and her vitality. Elsie's morning activities could easily encompass chopping wood for the stove, doing the weekly wash and ironing – activities that Stanley later celebrated in a series of Scrapbook Drawings. In fact Elsie was the perfect housewife that he wished to see in Hilda. He began to make unfavourable comparisons between the two. Why was Hilda always so tired? Why did she have no sense of time-keeping? Why was she so unpredictable? Stanley might come home at lunchtime exhausted and hungry, wanting to share a meal with Hilda, only to find that she had gone for a walk with Shirin or was in the garden digging a celery trench. And why did gardening take apparent precedence to painting?

In letters Stanley accuses Hilda of 'ceasing to paint and draw'. He writes to her that she 'can't expect to have any harmony ... between us when to my symphonic efforts you keep up a dreary beating of old tin cans which is all your sewing & gardening means to me'.[31] In fairness, Stanley's harsh comment reflects the great admiration that he always had for Hilda's work. He wants Hilda to paint but does not know how to support her in it. It is evident that his constant criticisms only made it more difficult for Hilda at this time to feel confident, settled and therefore productive. Hilda writes that 'my whole idea of Art and production is of an epic order & to produce an epic one's thoughts & convictions have to be positive and vital'.[32] During the spring and summer of 1928 Hilda could only find escape from her growing langour and listlessness in gardening. It was in effect her lifeline. 'To a creative person making things of some sort or kind is essential' wrote Hilda. At least in gardening there was 'something that is to be expressed'.[33] Hilda's crisis of expression however was symptomatic of a deeper unease born of a philosophy of life which challenged the significance of everyday human activity in general. Hilda's sincerely held Christian Science beliefs deemed the existence of the everyday physical world to be ultimately illusory. It seemed to Hilda that in her art she had been struggling to imitate that illusion and thus was being untruthful. To make matters worse, it bothered Hilda that Stanley's own equally strong religious beliefs were not informed by those of Christian Science. Although Hilda and Stanley shared an understanding of God as the essential ground of being, they could not reconcile their very different systems of beliefs as being manifestations of the will of that ultimate ground. To Hilda, God's presence could only be experienced on the 'spiritual' plane, as it was transcendent to the everyday illusionary world. By contrast, Stanley's God was simply 'The Thing Which Is', daily and necessarily experienced as imminent within physical reality. Thus to Stanley every act and entity became sacramental, and in a sense, God became incarnate in the very act of painting. All moods and states of mind were in this sense alike, equally divine. Perhaps because of this belief, Stanley possessed the unusual facility of being able to continue painting through periods of emotional turmoil and even intense physical pain. When suffering acutely from gallstones Stanley still kept painting in the Chapel.

By the end of 1928 Hilda had grown so wretched at their deteriorating relationship – 'more hopeless this time than ever before – much much more' – that she realized they needed to spend some time apart if their marriage was to survive. The family spent Christmas 1928 together at Downshire Hill after which Hilda stayed in Hampstead with Shirin while Stanley returned alone to Burghclere. During this separation they wrote long letters to each other, both recognizing that it was 'easier thinking things out away from each other for a while', the reason being that in this way they were not 'bothered by the untrue aspects of each other'. Away from Stanley, Hilda did indeed find it easier to express her anger and resentment – 'why don't you look into other people's minds and even size up what *they* may be feeling or what *their* impulse is, or *their need* is. Why do you work everything round about yourself as though you were the magnet round which everything worked & you were the motive for every action'.[34] After such outbursts Stanley admits to 'almost not wanting things to come right'. But gradually his love for Hilda began to resurface. 'Sometimes I feel impossible difficulties about you but other times quite welling over with happiness & joy at the thought of all the possibility of life and joy that you suggest'.[35] Just as Hilda began to feel 'much happier ... more hopeful and more powerful',[36] she suffered a huge personal blow with the death of her brother Sydney. On the evening of 14 February 1929, Hilda, Richard and their mother had been at the private view of Sydney's first one-man show in London, rejoicing at his success. Three days later he was dead, killed by the pneumonia caught, his family always maintained, during the freezing hours he had spent mending his car which had broken down on the road back to his home in Drayton St Leonard.[37] This was the Oxfordshire village where he had moved the previous summer after marrying an actress, Gwen Harter. Hilda had lost a second brother, a close friend and confidant.

After Sydney's death, Hilda found it difficult to even think of returning to Burghclere. She felt her place at this sad time was to remain with her mother. Stanley too was greatly moved by his brother-in-law's death. Its suddenness no doubt emphasized to both Hilda and Stanley their own mortality and encouraged them to think more positively about their own relationship 'not muddling each other's atmosphere'. Now Hilda received letters in which Stanley contemplated 'how completely possible our life may become together' and looked forward to her return – a return which must have been as joyful and loving as the welcome Hilda received in Stanley's well-known painting *Hilda welcomed*.[38]

Becoming conscious once again of Stanley's love for her, Hilda began to feel more confident in herself and optimistic about their future. She found it possible once again to take up her brushes. In the summer of 1929, partly to give Hilda's mother a break from Hampstead and partly so that Stanley could spend some time with his sister Annie who was showing symptoms of mental instability, Hilda and Stanley with Shirin and Hilda's mother and brother Richard spent six weeks in Cookham. Hilda began to respond to this different landscape. Holiday snapshots of this period show Hilda absorbed in painting. No pictures can be identified with certainty as being painted during this stay in Cookham, though it is possible that Hilda painted the expansive *Swans, Cookham Bridge* (cat.45) on this visit. This is a remarkable achievement given her lack of practice over the last four years. Hilda's painting is dominated by the wide-spanned, metal bridge over the Thames which gave an important focus to life in Cookham. As such it had already featured in one of Stanley's important early paintings, the now famous *Swan upping, Cookham*.[39] Stanley's picture strongly depends on personal association: it is an amalgam of imagination and reality, memory and observation. Hilda's picture, by contrast, is a more traditional, naturalistic vista. Attracted by the peace and tranquillity of the late summer scene, Hilda has set up her easel in Turk's boatyard and painted the scene just as it appears before her. As if in recognition of their rejuvenated relationship and of the great significance of this place for Stanley, Hilda painted one of her loveliest landscapes. No one is in a hurry in Hilda's picture. The unimpeded swans gently drift down the river and gather by the bank; the inhabitants of Cookham go about their business in leisurely fashion. The two horses slowly pull their heavily laden carts over the bridge; the young child with her mother and friend have stopped to watch the swans below, just as does the young cyclist leaning on his elbow and contemplating the late summer tranquility. Hilda chose the same elongated format as she had for her last landscape *Smoke from the Southwold train, Wangford* (cat.41) painted four years previously. As before she achieves a confidently balanced handling of space.

On her return to Burghclere, in the autumn of 1929, Hilda painted another significant work, a magnificent portrait of their maid Elsie (cat.43). She stands, dressed in her best clothes, in front of the kitchen range – queen of the Spencers' domestic domain. It is Elsie herself who is responsible for the calm order of the painting. She has swept the floor, neatly arranged the chair, filled the coal bucket, polished the fender, washed the clothes that hang drying above the range, dusted and tidied the jars and tins on the mantelpiece (which Hilda has detailed in a series of delightful still-lifes). Nothing though, distracts from the powerful presence of Elsie herself. With justification Stanley told Hilda, 'the way you have painted Elsie's skirt is a revelation to me'.[40] Stanley kept Hilda's painting of Elsie with him until he died. He also painted a portrait of Elsie at the same time as Hilda. Returning one day from the Sandham Chapel and finding Hilda busy painting Elsie, he too felt inspired, and set up his easel behind Hilda. With his view of Elsie partly obscured by Hilda, Stanley's portrait is a less ambitious work concentrating upon Elsie's head and shoulders, but it is an equally affectionate image of their valued servant.[41] Hilda followed up this portrait of Elsie by painting one of her mother (cat.46), in the drawing room at 47 Downshire Hill. This time Hilda has chosen to concentrate on the head and shouders and only hinted at the background detail. All attention is focused on the artist's mother whom she presents frankly as aging yet still formidable; the image of a sad but determined woman who stoically conceals the anguish of her losses – her husband and two of her sons making it necessarily a sombre picture. Its uncompromising realism contrasts

Hilda painting at Odney Common, Cookham, 1929

STANLEY SPENCER
Country girl: Elsie
1929, oil on canvas, dimensions unknown
Private collection

Portrait of the artist's mother
1930 (cat.46)
Oil on canvas, 710 × 610mm
Private collection

with the sensitive portrait Hilda made of her mother, *Melancholy in a country garden* (cat.25). It was painted a decade earlier, in the summer of 1921, a few months after the sudden death of her father.[42] Hilda and her mother were staying in Muirhead Bone's house in the tiny village of Steep near Petersfield, Hampshire. In this earlier painting Hilda's mother stands alone and forlorn, admidst the luxuriant abundance of the early summer garden, gazing through the open gate to the sunlit fields; a world beyond. It is a deeply expressive painting, reflecting Hilda's own grief, as well as her mother's. An overwhelming sense of sadness pervades the picture which nevertheless reveals the promise of a brighter future. By contrast there is no redeeming optimism in the 1930 portrait.

Back in Hampstead in the spring of 1930 Hilda was attempting to gain solace for another grief: the threatened breakdown once again of her relationship with Stanley. She was struggling with her realization that Stanley seemed only to want her as a

Melancholy in a country garden
1921 (cat.25)
Oil on canvas, 660 × 698mm
Private collection

Portrait of Shirin
1931 (cat.48)
Oil on canvas, 420 × 317mm
Private collection

personage defined and moulded by himself. He told her frankly that 'with everything you do & think I have got to feel in myself a possibility of *doing the same myself*'.[43] The 'same thing' extended to Hilda's paintings: it was not enough for Stanley to admire Hilda's paintings, he wanted to be part of her creative process as well. That a husband and wife, who were also both painters, should wish to express their affection for their maid Elsie in portrait is natural enough. However, it seemed, whenever Hilda painted a picture or suggested an idea, Stanley felt compelled to paint it as well. Hilda talked at this time of wishing to paint a double portrait of Stanley and herself. Stanley responded by saying he too wanted to attempt the same subject 'as it might show the differences and similarities of each other's atmosphere'.[44] Stanley was in danger of setting too much store by his feelings for Hilda as an artist: 'In your painting I can understand & love you & see how and where you and I are joined together.'[45]

Ultimately, Stanley's love for Hilda was based on more than his feelings for her as an artist, but his insistence on the importance of Hilda painting at a time when Hilda was struggling to find the emotional and physical space in which to work had disastrous consequences. In the spring of 1930, having at last managed to re-engage seriously with her work, she was determined to continue with it and so fled to Hampstead in an attempt to preserve the integrity of her personal vision. Hilda also needed time to think about how her conjugal life might be arranged after May when their second child was due to be born. On 24 May, Stanley received a telegram: 'Girl arrived 3.10am. Both splendid. Love. Writing. Hilda.' Their daughter was named Unity and two months later Hilda journeyed with the baby to Burghclere. It seems that over the next year or so nothing fundamental changed in Hilda and Stanley's relationship.

Hilda with Unity, 1930

There were obviously moments of love and tenderness recorded in an intimate series of pencil drawings that Hilda and Stanley made of each other in 1931. These nude studies (cat.47 and 69) are sensitively handled with soft outlines and delicate shading. Stanley also draws Hilda wearing only her long strand of beads and yet another time with her hair down, revelling in the 'wonderful feeling of infiniteness and endlessness' long hair gave him. Sadly such moments of tenderness when the Spencers entered 'into each other's atmosphere' could not endure. Before long, everyday tensions and irritations resurfaced. Hilda and Stanley had now been married for six years and had reached a stalemate in their relationship, unable to resolve their differences. Over the next six years they would reach a resolution but it proved to be messy and intensely hurtful.

The year 1931 brought about changes of a different nature. Stanley was now talking of a possible return to his beloved Cookham. He was at last coming towards the end of his great cycle of paintings in the Sandham Chapel. Since his highly successful 1927 show in London, the demand for Stanley's pictures had steadily grown. In 1929 the Empire Marketing Board had commissioned Stanley to produce a series of five paintings on the theme of Industry and Peace and during the previous four years at Burghclere, Stanley had received an increasing flow of portrait and landscape commissions. He was obviously greatly pleased by the assured source of income these commissions represented, but it was ideas for a major new cycle of visionary paintings that really engaged Stanley's thoughts and imagination during his long days of labour in the chapel. The new visionary paintings constituted a Church House project which was to be considerably more ambitious than his current chapel venture. Its aims were universal, to fix all his feelings and beliefs in the attempt to find a meaningful synthesis of the divine and the secular, the corporeal body of desire and the mind's spiritual yearning. Stanley hoped that through the Church House the gulf between innocence and experience would be bridged; sensuality redeemed and spiritual harmony attained. Having been fortunate in finding a patron for his war paintings in Sandham Chapel, he lived in the unrealistic hope that he would find similar patronage for this second immense and unconventional project. The hope alone gave shape and form to the rest of his life's work. From the start Stanley conceived the inter-relationships of the various parts of the Church House as reflecting the layout of his beloved Cookham – the nave was the main High Street, the crossroads at the top of the village, the transepts and so forth. With this grand scheme so informed by his 'Cookham feelings' Stanley felt compelled to reside once again in the village. Hilda could not feel as enthusiastic about the idea of living in Cookham and preferred them to return to London. Cookham obviously did not hold the same associations and meaning for her as for her husband and she knew that Stanley sensed her ambivalence. Indeed, over the last few years Stanley had grown to describe many of his feelings for Hilda as 'being antagonistic to my Cookham feelings' and doubted that Hilda 'could ever fit into (them)'. Hilda realized that it would be counterproductive to attempt to frustrate Stanley's deep desire to return to his native village and so, in the

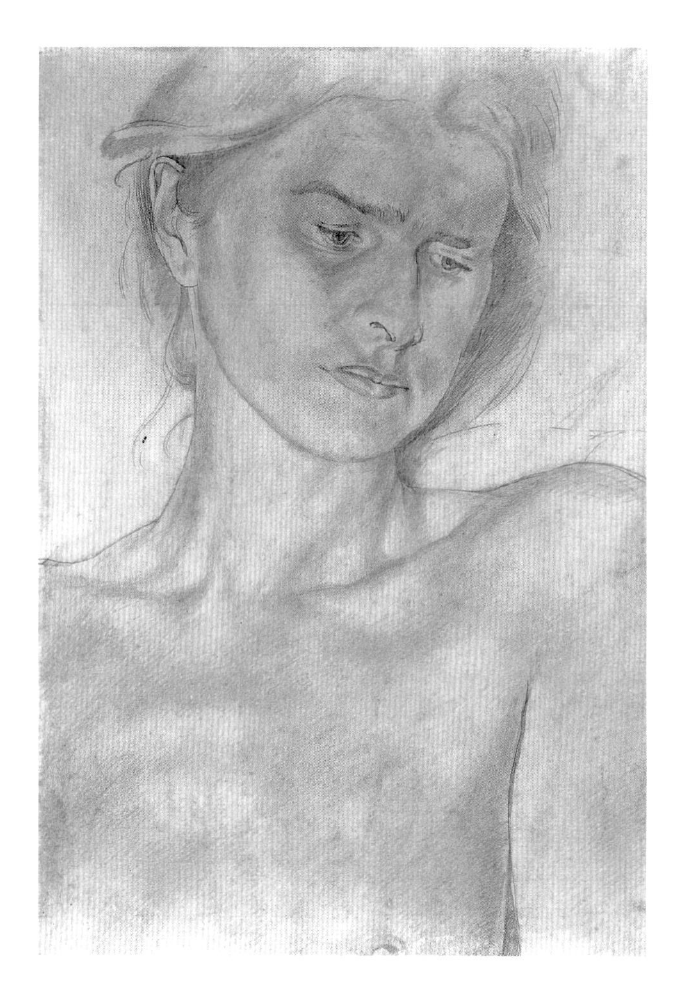

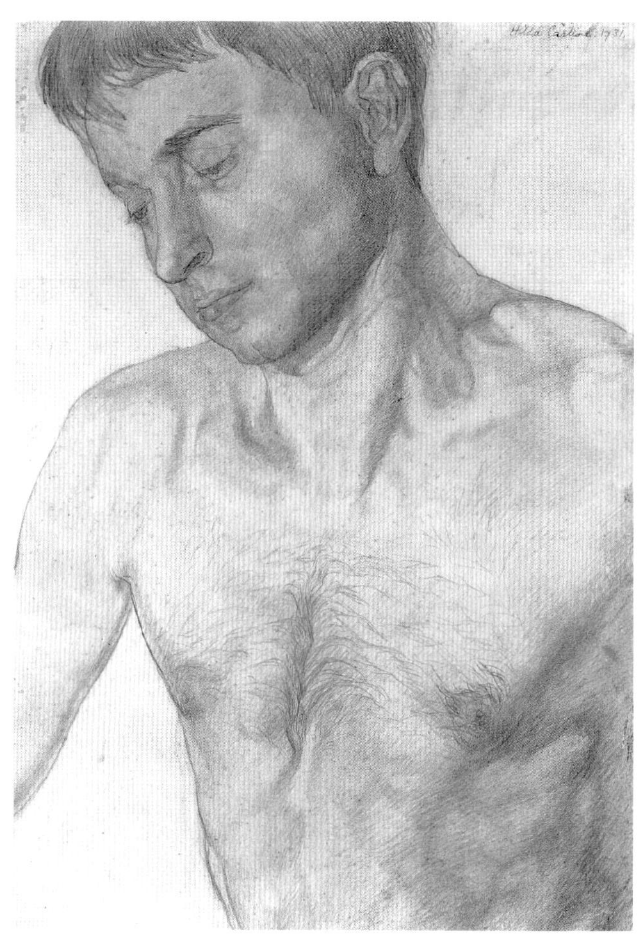

STANLEY SPENCER
Hilda nude
1931 (cat.69)
Pencil drawing, 508 × 352mm
National Galleries of Scotland

Stanley nude
1931 (cat.47)
Pencil drawing, 508 × 353mm
National Galleries of Scotland

autumn of 1931, Hilda accompanied Stanley there on several house-hunting visits. They eventually decided to buy Lindworth, a large and secluded semi-detached house in the middle of the village. On 21 January 1932, Stanley was at last able to return and take up residence in a substantial house in the heart of the village of his childhood, as a successful artist who soon became something of a local celebrity receiving invitations to 'the right sort of parties' and other village events. Hilda by contrast arrived in the village full of a strong sense of foreboding which was to prove all too prophetically and tragically correct.

Two summers previously, in 1929, when Hilda and Stanley had stayed for some weeks in Cookham with Hilda's mother and brother, Richard, they had met and made friends with Patricia Preece and Dorothy Hepworth who lived together in Moor Thatch Cottage in the village. Patricia and Dorothy were both painters who had trained, like Hilda and Stanley, at the Slade. They made a modest living from their work but, unbeknown to Hilda and Stanley or indeed anyone at the time, this was as the result of a highly unusual painting partnership. Dorothy painted the pictures, portraits, still-lifes and scenes of Cookham, while Patricia signed them and sold them as her own work. Dorothy was much the better painter of the two women, but she was also painfully shy and shrank away from any form of public recognition or the socialising necessary to build up a circle of appreciative patrons and critics of her work. Dorothy was quite happy to leave such things to the much more confident Patricia Preece.

Early in their business partnership, Patricia gained the support of Roger Fry who introduced her to other Bloomsbury artists, including Vanessa Bell and Duncan Grant, and more importantly for Patricia, their dealers. The result was that in the late 1920s and 1930s 'Patricia Preece' paintings were well known in London art circles and sufficiently highly regarded for no less than Augustus John to proclaim Patricia Preece as one of the six greatest living English women painters, taking precedence over even his own sister, Gwen John. There were naturally a few awkward situations for Patricia as when, for example, she was asked to accept portrait commissions, but somehow Patricia and Dorothy worked through the problems and the arrangement continued throughout their lives, and was even maintained posthumously after Patricia died! Patricia was hopeful, therefore, during the summer of 1929 that her new acquaintanceship with Stanley Spencer and his London-based brother-in-law (Richard Carline) would lead to helpful contacts and aid the duo in selling work. In the event both Stanley and Richard were more responsive to Patricia's glamorous appearance than to 'her' work. Probably to both Stanley and Richard, beside Hilda's work, 'Patricia's' paintings would have seemed merely competent, lacking Hilda's originality and intensity of vision.

Richard Carline's interest in Patricia ceased soon after he realized the likely lesbian nature of Patricia's relationship with Dorothy, which Stanley does not seem to have appreciated, or ever acknowledged. As soon as Hilda and Stanley moved to Cookham in January 1932, Stanley began to see Patricia on an almost daily basis. He was mesmerised by her: his fascination soon grew into infatuation, even obsession. Patricia became identified in Stanley's eyes with an important aspect of his 'Cookham feelings'. This was signified to Stanley by the fact that she and Dorothy chose to come to live in Cookham in 1928, since the village represented to Patricia one of the few happy periods of her childhood. Almost immediately Stanley began to make unfavourable comparisons between Patricia and Hilda. Patricia was stylish and elegant in a way Hilda was not. Patricia was direct and forceful while Hilda was complex, thoughtful – and circumspect. Patricia would welcome him at Moor Thatch Cottage and encourage him to expand on his views on art, literature and love. Hilda would grow bored, even doze off in the middle of some of Stanley's soliloquies (she had by now heard them many times before!). Patricia was socially sophisticated whereas Hilda was indifferent to, and even awkward at social gatherings. Stanley began to regard Patricia as, in some sense, necessary to the realization of his Church House ideas. He also wanted *her*, eventually as his wife, or at least as an additional wife!

Hilda was naturally greatly alarmed and disturbed by this new and unexpected turn of events. Initially she stayed in Cookham hoping that Stanley's interest in Patricia was a passing infatuation, and, strangely enough, she found that she did not dislike Patricia personally. She offered Patricia friendship, frequently visiting Patricia and Dorothy at Moor Thatch Cottage or taking excursions as a trio with Stanley and Patricia. Hilda was determined to keep open channels of communication with her husband. She also felt compassion for Patricia and Dorothy's obvious and increasing poverty. Retrospectively, Hilda came to believe that Patricia and Dorothy's lack of money, more than any other factor, precipitated the break-up of her marriage with Stanley. In 1939 she was to write, 'I am sure that Patricia had one thought only in her mind and that was to get the money and, finding Stanley a possible person, she set about to procure him, trying to keep the road clear to get rid of him when she wanted to.'[46] A dispassionate analysis of unfolding events would seem to bear out her observation.

In November 1930 Dorothy's father had died and was discovered to be bankrupt, having lost his fortune in the 1929 economic crash. Until then Dorothy and Patricia had relied on a regular monthly cheque from Dorothy's father to supplement their income and to make the mortgage repayments for Moor Thatch Cottage. Following his death the two women faced financial ruin and possible homelessness. Fortunately Dorothy's mother had a small private income and for a while struggled to keep up the mortgage repayments but the threat hung over the two women of Dorothy's mother foreclosing on their mortgage. The economic depression of the early 1930s did not help in selling 'Patricia's' paintings. It was at this difficult time that Patricia became aware of Stanley's attraction towards her, a man in markedly better material circumstances than her own. Here was an artist whose work she did not much like or even comprehend (indeed Patricia admired Hilda's work more than Stanley's), and yet who was making a comfortable income which enabled him to buy a fine house and fill it with beautiful art books and gramophone records. There obviously seemed to be 'money to spend'. Some of this surplus could easily stave off Patricia and Dorothy's looming financial ruin. Confident of Stanley's interest in her, Patricia appeared to have made the conscious decision to exploit his fascination. If this was the case it was a dangerous game to play, cynically encouraging Stanley's attentions whilst her emotional commitment remained solely to Dorothy.

Patricia accepted Stanley's wooing with apparent enthusiasm, receiving Stanley 'half or a quarter dressed, with perhaps a dressing gown on' and 'daring him to kiss her and, when he did not do so, said he was only a c3 man'.[47] Initially Stanley was nonplussed by Patricia's seeming openness and was consequently unsure of his own feelings towards her – which he would then endlessly analyse with, of all people, Hilda! As a result of these discussions feelings of great hopelessness and even despair began to overwhelm Hilda once again, but this time her response to her situation was less passive and she grew determined to fight for the survival of her marriage. In her struggle Hilda drew great strength from her profound faith in the doctrines of Christian Science. These teachings encouraged Hilda to believe that her suffering was only an artificial construct of her own mind. She decided to stay in Cookham instead of fleeing to London as she had done during the last crisis. However, during the summer of 1932, Hilda's brother George became seriously ill with heart disease. He was brought home to Downshire Hill from Halifax in Yorkshire where he had become Head of the Bankside Museum. As autumn passed, it looked increasingly unlikely that he would recover. With painful memories of Sydney's recent death still fresh upon her, Hilda felt her place was now at her brother's bedside with her mother, whatever her own personal circumstances. Hilda was well aware of the enormous risk to her relationship with Stanley that she took by leaving Cookham at this time, but she felt that she had to put her mother and brother first. George died on Christmas Eve. The few letters that Hilda had received from Stanley during her absence and their unusual tone told Hilda all she needed to know about the state of affairs in Cookham. Hilda was never again to reside permanently at Lindworth.

For the next eighteen months Hilda made regular, though increasingly short visits to Cookham. She took Unity, still only a toddler of three years, with her but made other arrangements for Shirin. In previous years, at difficult times, her brother Sydney's mother-in-law, Mrs Harter, who lived in Hampstead close to Downshire Hill, had helped Hilda by having Shirin to stay with her. Now that Shirin was of school age, Mrs Harter suggested that she live with her and attend a local school. As much as Hilda hated splitting up Shirin and Unity and missed Shirin desperately, she felt she had no option but to accept Mrs Harter's offer, though she clung to the hope that Stanley's infatuation with Patricia might subside and they could all live together again. At the same time, anxious not to put undue pressure on Stanley, she writes:

> 'I am tremendously anxious for the right thing to happen, and for you to have what you need and want. I am so much more anxious for that, than that I should have any of my personal wants. Although I have a lot of personal wants they have not been actuating me in this affair because I much more want everyone's happiness than just my own'.[48]

It is tempting to think that the occasional outburst from Hilda might have better served her ultimate desire for Stanley to abandon Patricia, but she perhaps realized from the experience of the past eight years that their marriage could never work unless Stanley desired a reunion and returned to her voluntarily.

Needless to say, with all the domestic turmoils and uncertainities about her own future, Hilda found it impossible to sustain any long-term involvement in her work and just two paintings date from 1933. In the summer, Hilda took Shirin and Unity for a holiday to Wangford. Glad to be away from both London and Cookham and to be back in the setting of happier memories Hilda painted an impressive outdoor composition, *Children with toys* (cat.50), in which Shirin and Unity appear twice. Given the heaviness of Hilda's heart, it is a surprisingly light and airy painting with its observation of the play of dappled summer light diffusing through the softly painted trees. There are no such delicate touches in the extraordinary portrait that Hilda painted at the end of that year. With heavy energetic strokes Hilda constructed the features of none other than Patricia in *Lady in green* (cat.49), dragging her brush across the forehead in, as it were, a great frown. It is almost impossible to imagine how, at this time of obviously worsening relationships between Hilda and Stanley and knowing that she was the cause of them, that Patricia ever agreed to sit for Hilda – and that Hilda wanted, or was willing, to paint the 'blonde temptress' of her husband. Stanley maintains in his 1933 Day Book that the portrait was his idea and that he 'set' Hilda to paint Patricia. Certainly Hilda came to Cookham a few days before Christmas 1933 and spent her time painting Patricia. Perhaps Hilda was simply curious about this woman who exerted such power over her husband and who had replaced herself as Stanley's 'muse'. On her visits to Lindworth, Hilda would have seen for example, Stanley's recent paintings *The meeting* (1932) and *Separating fighting swans* (1933): new interpretations of his old 'Cookham feelings' in which his early youthful feelings of spiritual exaltation have become clearly charged with his adult sexual ideals personified in the images of Patricia which the works contain.[49] Hilda would also have seen, and perhaps been surprised by, Stanley's own portrait of Patricia painted earlier that year (1933).[50] Where was the 'peculiar excrutiatingly exquisiteness' he proclaimed that he saw in Patricia? Instead we see a woman with heavy, rather unattractive features and large awkward hands, leaning inelegantly on a table. Hilda's painting is of a much more refined and attractive woman. Drawing upon all her reserves and skills as an artist, Hilda has perhaps concentrated the intensity of her feelings of despair and rejection in this portrait of her rival who, under the scrutiny of Hilda's gaze has to look away, perhaps guiltily, perhaps beginning to realize the consequence of her actions.

Hilda, Shirin and Unity
Southwold, 1933

Hilda made visits to Cookham in the January and the March of 1934 to finish her painting of Patricia but the act of making this portrait confirmed to her that there was no longer any obvious place for her in Stanley's life. In May she removed her own possessions to Hampstead. Having lost Stanley, Hilda initially sought to make sense of the situation through her painting. With a brief burst of energy she painted the familar *Downshire Hill garden* (cat.51). From the picture's rich, dark focus of thick foliage a shower of spring blossom bursts forth. But Hilda could not maintain her absorption; she could not simply turn away from her enormous hurt and continue life unaffected. In a letter written the following spring, one glimpses the terrible despair and mood of utter bleakness that overwhelmed Hilda that summer of 1934 – both mentally and physically:

> 'In the summer my eyesight nearly went, I could not look at things as I walked along a road ... because the moving things hurt them & eventually made me unable to distinguish things ... Sometimes however I almost hoped to go out of my mind, as that I thought would break up my train of thought, & stop all recollections and puzzles or hopeless hopes & so on.'[51]

STANLEY SPENCER
Portrait of Patricia Preece
1933
Oil on canvas, 839 × 736mm
Southampton City Art Gallery

The fact that Hilda's hold on reality and self-worth was not completely crushed at this time is largely due to the concern and generosity of a long-time friend and admirer of her work, Fiske Warren, who at this critical time paid for Hilda and Unity to take a holiday in Switzerland; 'the best time I have had, in fact the only hopeful or happy time'.[52]

As well as the Swiss holiday lifting her spirits it must also have meant much to Hilda to know that someone had wanted to spend money on her. Hilda returned from Switzerland to face a new battle with Stanley – over maintenance payments. Ironically, Patricia (and Dorothy) now had sufficient money but Hilda extremely little. At the beginning of 1935 Stanley was proposing to reduce his contribution to her even further. In the year since Hilda had left him, Patricia's power over Stanley had reached its peak. In September 1934 Stanley bought Patricia her first piece of expensive jewellery, an eternity ring. Over the next two years he lavished jewellery and other gifts on her, including the deeds, and therefore the ownership, of Hilda and Stanley's Cookham home, Lindworth. The not too surprising result of this extravagance was that Stanley was rapidly sliding into major debt and now felt that he could not afford to pay Hilda her agreed maintenance. He complained to Hilda that he too had been ill (a major operation to remove gallstones), that he had lost a lot of commissions and preferred to spend what money he had on Patricia! Although Hilda was not in imminent danger of becoming homeless, as Patricia and Dorothy had been earlier, she had insufficient means to buy clothes and other essential items for Unity and herself. Shirin was still living with Mrs Harter who also needed to receive money. Hilda's increasingly desperate pleas to Stanley were intercepted by Patricia. Having successfully managed Dorothy and her own affairs, Patricia had taken on the role of Stanley's 'business manager', one of whom's prime duties included vetting much of Stanley's correspondence. At this time Stanley probably saw few of Hilda's letters.

Finally Hilda felt that she had no option but to institute legal proceedings to recover some money from Stanley. When these proved unsatisfactory and believing 'that it was impossible for you (Stanley) to pursue any course other than the one you were pursuing'[53] she filed for a divorce in 1936. Stanley's response to these new developments was, at an everyday level, to feel great anger towards Hilda at her actions but in his imagination to begin a process of recovering his early vision of her, an idealized vision that he would embroider and maintain for the rest of his life. In the imaginary world of his paintings he could mould and shape his image of Hilda to reflect his own emotion. Stanley began this 'resurrection' of Hilda with a glorified exaltation of their married life, his Domestic Series. In these he nostalgically recalls moments of especial joy and significance in conjugal life: the calm at the end of the day when Hilda and he were *Going to bed* or intimate acts such as Hilda *Taking off collar* or Stanley and Hilda *Choosing a petticoat* or *Choosing a dress* or selecting clothes *At the chest of drawers*.[54] While waiting for the Decree Nisi of their divorce to be ratified Stanley surprisingly painted his only nude of Hilda. He worked from the nude 'Hilda with Beads' drawing he made in 1931 and wrote during its production that 'we continue to be utterly at one, rejoicing in our oneness'.

Enjoying this resurgence of his love for Hilda but at the same time still wanting Patricia to share his visionary life, Stanley conceived the idea that Hilda, Patricia and himself should live together in a ménage à trois. Familiar with Hilda's traditional views on marriage, Stanley knew that it would take much time and great tact if there was to be any chance of persuading Hilda to accept such an arrangement. For the time being, therefore, he only dared to propose his plan to Patricia who, much to Stanley's satisfaction, readily agreed to co-operate. Patricia most likely saw in this proposal a way of retaining an interest in Stanley from which she could benefit materially while freeing herself from the distasteful sexual obligations to one of her probable orientation. Hilda would be available to Stanley instead. Thus Patricia agreed to marry Stanley only on condition that it was to be merely a legal formality with no co-habitation on her part implied until Hilda had agreed to take part in the ménage à trois. In the meantime Patricia devised her own scheme to manage the entire situation.

The Decree Absolute hearing for Hilda and Stanley's divorce was set for 25 May 1937 and Hilda knew that Patricia and Stanley planned to marry four days later. Hilda felt concerned about the maintenance agreement – could she rely on Stanley's continued payment given the difficulties of the past two years? Hilda received a letter form Patricia begging her not to delay her agreement to the decree as she had taken a cottage at St Ives in Cornwall for a month as a 'honeymoon' surprise for Stanley – 'if you will do this for us now Hilda so that it goes through as we have arranged for, we shall both remember it in the future and you shall not lose by it'[55] Patricia's letter also suggested that Hilda go to Lindworth to collect any of her personal belongings that she wanted. Hilda did not attempt to delay the Decree Absolute and a week later went to Lindworth and to her surprise found Stanley still there! Patricia and Dorothy had departed to begin the Cornish 'honeymoon' without Stanley who had to finish a landcape, the sale of which was to pay the wedding expenses. It was a highly emotionally charged situation. After much persuasion and assurance on Stanley's part that Patricia wanted her to spend the night at Lindworth, Hilda agreed to stay. Inevitably they slept in the same bed and their old intimacy was renewed. The next morning Stanley proposed his ménage à trois. Sadly Hilda realised that she 'had been beguiled by the whole atmosphere', but all the same 'I did not regret it, as that perfect day seemed to wipe away all the last few years and to have put things right between Stanley and me'.[56] On the contrary, the same events 'put all things wrong' between Stanley and Patricia. When he had completed his landscape, Stanley joined Patricia and Dorothy in Cornwall as planned, and, with characteristic candour, told Patricia of his night with Hilda. This was understandable in that Patricia had been apparently supportive of his ménage à trois plan. It would appear however that Patricia had manipulated Hilda's visit to Cookham in the calculated hope that it would yield the irrefutable excuse in law she wanted to never have to cohabit with Stanley. After Stanley's revelation the new husband and wife occupied separate rooms in St Ives, and once back in Cookham, Patricia and Dorothy continued living together at Moor Thatch Cottage and Stanley alone at Lindworth.

Hilda records that she returned to Hampstead from her momentous day in Cookham 'with rosy cheeks & sparkling eyes & happy with everyone, friendly &

kindly disposed to everyone, in fact in an ideal state'.[57] Such euphoria did not last. How *could* Stanley possibly expect her to happily become his mistress when she had once been his wife? For several months during the summer of 1937 Stanley persisted in trying to persuade Hilda to accept at least in essence, just such an arrangement. To this end he visited her in Hampstead. When Hilda still did not yield to his appeals he went off moodily to paint landscapes in Wangford hoping its associations with happier times might woo Hilda back to him. When Hilda did not join him, Stanley returned to Hampstead where he painted one of his most interesting and moving portraits – *Hilda, Unity and dolls* (cat.70).[58] Hilda is turned away, the strain of the past months and years visibly etched on her face. Unity, with the unerring candour of childhood, stares straight at her father, challenging him, seemingly, with a knowledge beyond her seven years. Evidently, Hilda's tense state and Unity's far-sighted gaze communicated themselves to Stanley more eloquently than could any words. When the painting was complete, Stanley packed his bags and returned, crushed, to Cookham. In the future he would attempt to persuade Hilda to live with him, but his immediate concerns were to sort out his disastrous marriage to Patricia and to fight off the threat of bankrupty with which two alimony requirements presented him.

Hilda always felt glad about the night of reconciliation with Stanley at Lindworth but she no longer had faith that they could 'pull together'. Indeed, during the previous couple of difficult years when she had felt 'completely cut off' from Stanley, Hilda had fought hard 'to reconstruct my life and thoughts' towards a state of non-reliance on her husband. She wanted to preserve this hard-won state of comparative emotional equilibrium. Moreover, there were other reasons that arose during the early summer of 1937 which encouraged Hilda to feel more confident and optimistic than she had felt for a long while. That summer the Carlines moved from 47 Downshire Hill to nearby 17 Pond Street. Hilda was delighted that at last she had some proper space of her own. Another aspect of her separation from Stanley that Hilda had found hard to bear had been the cramped conditions of her former home where 'all my possessions ... are packed into that tiny bedroom that has to accomodate Unity and me. I cannot even have my paintbox about, it has to be packed away'.[59] Nor could Unity have many of her toys. Now at Pond Street, Unity had her own room and Hilda had a large double room where she could have her paintbox and pictures around her. At the time of their move Hilda had been working on *Portrait of Unity* (cat.53) which she planned to finish and start all sorts of new work. Hilda even began to dare to hope that in the future she might have a place of her own where Shirin could come and live with Unity and herself. (Shirin was still residing with Mrs Harter who had moved from Hampstead to Epsom.)

STANLEY SPENCER
Hilda, Unity and dolls
1937 (cat.70)
Oil on canvas, 762 × 508mm
City Art Gallery, Leeds

Hilda's optimism at the time of her move to Pond Street was short-lived. Over the next five years she was to be assailed from all sides leading finally to that state for which she had half-longed at the height of her unhappiness three years earlier – the oblivion from reality gained at the cost of a breakdown. The first assault on her peace of mind took the form of Stanley's summer of appeals to Hilda to join a ménage à

Hilda in her room
Pond Street, Hampstead, 1937

Studio photograph of Hilda, 1940

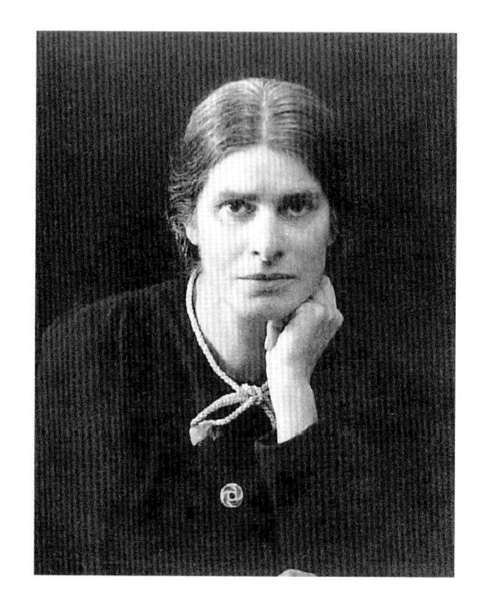

trois with Patricia and himself. Then followed an autumn and winter of bitter regrets that she had been wooed by Patricia away from her original resolve of delaying 'completion of the divorce till you had payed every farthing of what you owed'. Stanley was once again falling into arrears with maintenance payments. 'It's no good pretending that children can live on air'[60] she told Stanley on the eve of yet another hearing for recovery of unpaid maintenance. This time, however, it seems that Stanley really could not afford to pay Hilda. Stanley's two years' frenzy of luxurious spending on Patricia had left him seriously in debt. The court found in Hilda's favour but it was a hollow victory when Stanley did not have the resources to pay her. In the end it was Stanley's dealer, Dudley Tooth, rather than the lawyers who brought Hilda some succour. Part of Tooth's financial arrangements with Stanley included paying Hilda directly from Stanley's earnings at the gallery. He also offered Hilda space to exhibit her work in mixed exhibitions. Hilda was overjoyed at both proposals: 'I feel so grateful for the mental relief arising from this new system. It is a load off one's mind to feel that we can dispense with solicitors and such like'.[61] In the event, however, Hilda does not seem to have taken up Tooth's offer of gallery space, even though she had been exhibiting regularly at the Royal Academy during the second half of the 1930s in an

Portrait of Unity
1937 (cat.53)
Oil on board, 534 × 428mm
Private collection

attempt to ease her financial situation. Each year since 1935 Hilda had submiited a landscape with some success. For example, *Swans, Cookham Bridge* (cat.45) was bought by the Harris Museum, Preston in 1935 where it remains to the present day. Hilda at this time contemplated holding a solo show but, sadly, she did not possess either the mental or physical resources for the sustained effort needed to produce the necessary volume of work. To make matters worse, her fragile mental state was to be weakened still further by worries over events of the early years of the Second World War.

Throughout the 1930s Hilda had greatly valued Unity's supportive companionship. In 1939, fearing for her daughter's safety, Hilda agreed that Unity should go and live with Shirin and Mrs Harter in Epsom. There was a possibility that Hilda could have moved to Epsom too, but she confined herself to weekends and the occasional longer visit feeling that she ought to remain with her mother, who was now approaching her eightieth year, in Hampstead. Even after Unity's departure Hilda still felt worried by Epsom's close proximity to Croydon aerodrome, an obvious target for German bombers. During a visit in 1941 to Shirin and Unity these fears were realized: a jettisoned bomb destroyed a neighbouring house. This event, though, spurred Hilda into major decisions over the future of her daughters. For a while she had suspected that Unity was not happy in Epsom; she also felt concerned about the quality of the children's schooling. She wanted Shirin and Unity to have the opportunity of a broader and more progressive education than was available locally. Hilda visited several possible schools and eventually decided on Badminton School which had been evacuated to the Tors Hotel, Lynmouth for the duration of the war. On the basis of Shirin's gift for music and Unity's for art, the school offered them essential bursaries. Although Shirin and Unity were keen for this new educational experience, Hilda had not anticipated Mrs Harter's vehement opposition to her plans. Mrs Harter was, understandably, upset at the prospect of losing the two girls. Unexpectedly, Stanley supported Mrs Harter. Hilda dug in her heels, but at the same time felt distraught at this new difference of opinion between Stanley and herself. It brought back to Hilda, with full force, her agonies over their disagreements in past years, confirming the impossibility of ever living happily with Stanley again. Hilda's feelings of isolation and desolation were compounded by her grief at the sudden loss of two close friends in the London Blitz. These deaths were perhaps the final catalyst to Hilda's complete breakdown. One night in June 1942 she woke up her mother and housekeeper Miss Arnfield with the delusion that they were all about to be murdered by Mrs Harter! That same night Hilda was admitted to St Pancras Hospital and soon after transferred to Banstead Mental Hospital, where she remained for nine months.

In retrospect, Hilda regarded her time at Banstead as meaningful in initiating a new closeness and understanding between Stanley and herself and in enabling her to reclaim her faith in God, lost during her tribulations of the 1930s. 'Some of my most wonderful memories', she later wrote to Stanley, 'are of those visits of yours to me in my little cell at Banstead. I used to be spending my entire time talking with God and contemplating & it was as though I came straight from Heaven to enjoy you when

Hilda and Stanley on a visit to see Shirin and Unity, Badminton School, Lynmouth, 1943

you came'.[62] Each Sunday afternoon Stanley made the tedious and difficult wartime journey from Cookham to Banstead to see Hilda. During his visits they would enjoy long talks or read aloud from long unposted letters which they had written to each other during the preceding week. Without doubt Stanley was profoundly moved by Hilda's breakdown, blaming himself and his actions for his part in it. Stanley was now perhaps more sympathetic to Hilda's situation than he might have been had her breakdown occurred a decade earlier, for Stanley had also recently experienced a depressive state himself. This had begun early in 1939 at a time when he could forsee no realistic hope of a reconciliation with Hilda. He was also now estranged from Patricia who had evicted him from his former home! In addition to these miseries he was greatly financially encumbered and was forced to flee to a sparsely furnished room in Adelaide Road, Hampstead. There he found personal solace and renewed inspiration in reading and contemplating the stories of the Bible. One result of this intense period of meditation was his *Christ in the wilderness* series which can be seen to reflect both Christ's and his own sufferings.[63] In the event only eight of a total of forty preparatory sketches were worked up into finished canvases which provide a moving insight into his state of mind at this time. Stanley's later description of his own 'temptation in the wilderness' bears an uncanny similarity with Hilda's reported feelings at Banstead. Stanley, too, had found 'something wonderful in the life I was living my way into, penetrating into the unknown me ... I loved it all because it was God and me all the time.'[64]

Just as Stanley had found a vehicle for the expression of his tumultuous emotions in his *Christ in the wilderness* series of paintings, so Hilda's intense period of meditation at Banstead resulted in a moving series of pastel drawings. Hilda's daughter Shirin recalls her mother telling her how these pastels were intended to evoke something of the mood of the religious poetry of Mary Baker Eddy, the foundress of the Christian Science movement. Indeed taken as a group, the ten small and two large pastels might be seen to mirror Mary Baker Eddy's joyful celebration of God's creation and her hope for the life to come. They also contain something of the pain of Hilda's long separation from her children. In each of the small pastels is a young child, Shirin or Unity, clad simply in a short white tunic dancing in a woodland glade or playing a lyre to a golden oriole singing in the branches of a tree above or again, happily splashing in a mountain stream. Hilda depicts significant moments of their early childhood. The child raptuously contemplating the pure white flowers in the grass is Shirin who one day as a baby, had knelt on all fours gazing in just this manner into the long grass. This simple act of reverence had obviously greatly moved both Hilda and Stanley simultaneously. When Stanley painted Christ *Considering the lilies*, Christ too is kneeling, Shirin-style, in similar rapt adoration.

Hilda's two larger pastels are less overtly personal. In these she contends with a somewhat different issue – how to adapt her ideas about the four seasons to the apexed space for a 'fresco' at either ends of a large room (hence the triangular shape of the drawings (cat.57 and 58). The twelve pastels were in fact working sketches for a set

Luxembourg Gardens, Paris
1939 (cat.54)
Oil on canvas, 597 × 727mm
Private collection

of decorative wall panels for the main hall of a Social Club in Epsom! Such 'poetic' subjects do seem curiously inappropriate for such a venue. Hilda was not normally incapable of entering into the demands of specific briefs. Previously, just after the outbreak of the Second World War, she had successfuly designed a blackout blind for a firm of antique dealers in Westminster (cat.55): its eye-catching originality was such that it gained the notice of both the *Daily Telegraph* and *Morning Post*.[65] By 1943, the year of the pastels' composition, it became virtually impossible for Hilda to organise her thoughts in such a disciplined way. Perhaps her fresco designs might best be understood as an attempt at therapy – which also allowed Hilda's instinct for strong pure colour to reassert itself with all the intensity of her Tudor-Hart days. The dazzling emerald green and seering sky blue of these pastels recall the rich glowing colours of her works from that time, especially *A Fantasy* (cat.7) or *Zeppelin over London* (cat.9). Hilda's interest in pastel had been aroused by the gift to her of a box of pastel crayons from her brother Richard at Christmas 1939. Hilda drew a pair of Christmas lilies that very day and discovered an immediate sympathy for the medium. In the last few years before her breakdown she had used pastels for a series of portraits and freer, more imaginative compositions such as *Children in trees* and *Horses in the forest*. It seemed a natural step, therefore, to use pastel to express her religious *Children and nature* ideas (cat.59), and as a dramatic summary of her Christian beliefs, *A vision of God in heaven*, 1946 (cat.62). In this work the immensity of God's love and being blazes in a swirling incandescent ball of golden light from which revelational beams guide

Children and nature: study for a mural
*c.*1943 (cat.59)
Pastel, 150 × 180mm
Private collection

A boulevard in Paris
1946 (cat.60)
Oil on canvas, 355 × 268mm
Private collection

the eye to the series of Giotto-esque miniatures of Christ's Birth, Crucifixion, Resurrection and Ascension which range along the lower half of the drawing.

In November 1946 Hilda and Shirin visited Paris, as a celebration of Shirin's twenty-first birthday and also to attend the opening of the *Exposition Internationale d'Art Moderne* at the Musée d'Art Moderne which Hilda's brother Richard had organised in his capacity as first Art Counsellor of UNESCO. During her visit to the French capital Hilda painted two delightfully atmospheric Parisian street scenes (one of which can be seen in cat.60). For a while it seemed as if some of her early vigour and productivity had returned. But the bitter cold winter of 1946–7 proved a long and trying one for Hilda during which she felt increasingly unwell. In the spring of 1947 a lump was found in one of Hilda's breasts and a mastectomy was performed. The surgeon's prognosis was encouraging but Hilda's convalescence was long and slow and in fact she never regained her former strength. Throughout 1950 she fell victim to increasing pain and finally in October she was admitted to the Royal Free Hospital, Hampstead. There was now no hope of recovery. During Hilda's last days Stanley was constantly at her bedside but just ten minutes after Stanley had slipped out for brief refreshment at a nearby cafe, on the evening of Wednesday 1 November, 1950, Hilda died.

> 'I kiss the cross, and wake to know
> A world more bright.'[66]

On the face of it, a series of tragedies appear to make up Hilda and Stanley's joint history, but ultimately, the great love that they felt for each other might be said to have triumphed. The new understanding which began between Hilda and Stanley at

STANLEY SPENCER
Marriage at Cana
1953 (cat.74)
Oil on canvas, 660 × 510mm
Glynn Vivian Art Gallery, Swansea

STANLEY SPENCER
Hilda welcomed
*c.*1950
Oil on canvas, 1400 × 950mm
Art Gallery of Southern Australia, Adelaide

the time of Hilda's breakdown was maintained and enriched throughout the 1940s, drawing them ever closer as a couple. Stanley regularly visited Hilda in Hampstead and throughout the late 1940s, Hilda made occasional reciprocal visits to Stanley in his new home at Clivedon View, Cookham. There was even some talk of remarriage and after Hilda's operation, Stanley initiated proceedings towards an annulment of his marriage to Patricia on the grounds that the marriage had not been consummated. Hilda's death cut short this scheme which probably had little chance of success. Instead Stanley now sought union with Hilda on a spiritual level. The decade following Hilda's death, up until his own death in 1959, witnessed Stanley's transfiguration of his relationship with Hilda. In a sense, this process had already begun in the 1930s with his Domestic Series. One result of Hilda's death was to rekindle Stanley's interest in his original Church House project. In the 1930s Stanley had intended that the central part of the Church House would contain a series of paintings on the theme of the gospel story of the *Marriage at Cana* (cat.71). This symbolized both the physical and spiritual aspects of marriage which to Stanley was the principal sacrament of life. In 1953 he painted the key picture of the series, *Bride and bridegroom*, showing the newly weds (Hilda and Stanley) at their own marriage feast: a symbol of God's divine blessing on his spiritual union with Hilda.[67] For the rest of his life Stanley endlessly mused on Hilda and the course of their love, rereading their letters to each other, writing fresh ones to Hilda and recreating on canvas significant events from their life together. Memories of their courtship on Hampstead Heath inspired *Hilda with bluebells*. Family life gave rise to *Hilda and I at Burghclere*. Stanley also recalled the distressing times of Hilda's recent illness as in *Hilda and I at Pond Street*, where Hilda is depicted collapsed into her chair, with cushions pushed in the hollow of her back in an attempt to ease her pain. These paintings together with his earlier Domestic Series, were planned to cover the walls of a special Hilda Chapel in his Church House for which he began, but never finished, a huge celebratory altar piece, *The Apotheosis of Hilda*,[68] in which Hilda repeatedly appears. Although Stanley died before he could finish it this painting may be regarded as the crowning celebration of Hilda and Stanley's love:

> LOVE, thou art Absolute sole Lord
> OF LIFE & DEATH.[69]

ENDNOTES

1 Tate Gallery Archives (TGA) 8022.55, p.10
2 ibid p.10
3 ibid p.10
4 ibid p.11
5 ibid p.11
6 ibid p.12
7 ibid p.11
8 *The Cambridge Magazine*, 2 March 1918, p.480
9 *Stanley Spencer: A Hampstead Vision*, exh.cat. Burgh House, London, 1991, p.27
10 Gilbert Spencer, *Stanley Spencer by his Brother*, Victor Gollancz, London, 1961, p.164
11 John Rothenstein, *Stanley Spencer: the Man, Correspondence and Reminiscences*, Paul Elek, London, 1979, p.24
12 The location of this painting is presently unknown.
13 John Rothenstein, op.cit. p.24
14 Gilbert Spencer, op.cit. p.24
15 *Stanley Spencer at Burghclere* (introduction by Duncan Robinson), National Trust, 1991, p.3
16 For works by Stanley Spencer, refer to Keith Bell, *Stanley Spencer: A Complete Catalogue of the Paintings*, Phaidon Press, London, 1992, cited here as 'B' numbers: *Zacharias and Elizabeth*, B16; *The centurion's servant*, B21; *Mending cowls, Cookham*, B26
17 Keith Bell, op.cit. *Travoys arriving with wounded at a dressing station, Smol, Macedonia 1916*, B30
18 *Stanley Spencer* RA, exh.cat. Royal Academy, London, 1980, p.56
19 Keith Bell, op.cit. *River Nareta, Mostar*, B88
20 in Kenneth Pople, *Stanley Spencer: A Biography*, Collins, 1991, p.209
21 No pre-marriage letters survive from Hilda to Stanley
22 John Rothenstein, op.cit. p.27
23 ibid p.29
24 Kenneth Pople, op.cit. p.209
25 This self-portrait is in a private collection
26 Keith Bell, op.cit. *The Resurrection, Cookham*, B116
27 Maurice Collis, *Stanley Spencer*, Harvill Press, London, 1962, p.88
28 John Rothenstein, op.cit. p.39
29 Keith Bell, op.cit. *Trees and chicken coop, Wangford*, B114
30 Maurice Collis, op.cit. p.91
31 John Rothenstein, op.cit. p.39
32 TGA 8022.55, op.cit. p.4
33 ibid p.4
34 John Rothenstein, op.cit. p.33
35 ibid p.33
36 ibid p.33
37 Since 1922 Sydney Carline had been the Ruskin Master of Drawing at Oxford
38 Keith Bell, op.cit. *Hilda welcomed*, B384
39 *Swan upping, Cookham* is in the collection of the Tate Gallery, London; Keith Bell, op.cit. B27
40 John Rothenstein, op.cit. p.34
41 Keith Bell, op.cit. *Country girl: Elsie*, B129
42 Hilda spent the summer of 1920 painting in the Italian Alps with Sydney and Richard. In November they were journeying south with their parents when George Carline died suddenly of a heart attack at Assisi. See *Hillside, Assisi* (cat.22)
43 John Rothenstein, op.cit. p.34
44 ibid p.34
45 ibid p.34
46 ibid p.48
47 ibid p.48
48 ibid p.53
49 Keith Bell, op.cit. *The meeting*, B145; *Separating fighting swans*, B152
50 Keith Bell, op.cit. *Portrait of Patricia Preece*, B154
51 John Rothenstein, op.cit. p.54
52 ibid p.55
53 ibid p.56
54 Keith Bell, op.cit. *Going to bed*, B198; *Taking off collar*, B191; *Choosing a petticoat*, B194; *Choosing a dress*, B195; *At the chest of drawers*, B192
55 John Rothenstein, op.cit. p.61
56 Kenneth Pople, op.cit. p.363
57 John Rothenstein, op.cit. p.64
58 Keith Bell, op.cit. *Hilda, Unity and dolls*, B229
59 John Rothenstein, op.cit. p.55
60 ibid p.65
61 Kenneth Pople, op.cit. p.397
62 Hilda to Stanley Spencer, Tate Gallery Archives, TGA 733.1, p.1608
63 Keith Bell, op.cit. *Christ in the wilderness*, B283A–H
64 *Stanley Spencer* RA, op.cit. p.170
65 *Daily Telegraph* and *Morning Post*, 20 November 1939
66 From 'Christ my Refuge' in *Poems* by Mary Baker Eddy, Boston, USA, 1910
67 Keith Bell, op.cit. *Bride and bridegroom*, B385
68 *Hilda with bluebells*, *Hilda and I at Burghclere*, *Hilda and I at Pond Street* and *The Apotheosis of Hilda* are all in private collections
69 Richard Crashaw, quoted in *Stanley Spencer: The Apotheosis of Love*, exh.cat. Barbican Art Gallery, London, 1991, p.9

A Fantasy
1914 (cat.7)
Oil on canvas, 382 × 485mm
Private collection

Return from the farm
1919 (cat.17)
Oil on canvas, 1300 × 910mm
Private collection

Cliffs, Seaford
1920 (cat.19)
Oil on canvas, 1102 × 622mm
Private collection

Hillside, Assisi
1920 (cat.22)
Water-colour, 280 × 378mm
Private collection

Lake Orta
1920 (cat.24)
Oil on canvas, 420 × 555mm
Private collection

Count Tossa's children
1921 (cat.23)
Oil on canvas
1285 × 865mm
Private collection

Standing female nude
1922 (cat.27)
Oil on canvas, 750 × 500mm
Private collection

Woman in a red hat
1922 (cat.29)
Oil on canvas, 606 × 480mm
Private collection

Wooden minaret
1922 (cat.33)
Oil on canvas, 380 × 293mm
Private collection

Donkeys, Sarajevo
1922 (cat.34)
Oil on canvas, 292 × 292mm
Private collection

Portrait of Stanley Spencer
1923 (cat.38)
Oil on canvas, 610 × 458mm
Private collection

Self-portrait
1923 (cat.39)
Oil on canvas, 749 × 578mm
Tate Gallery, London

Smoke from the Southwold train, Wangford
1925 (cat.41)
Oil on canvas, 335 × 865mm
Private collection

Elsie
1929 (cat.43)
Oil on canvas, 1727 × 813mm
The Brighton & Hove Collections

Lady in green (portrait of Patricia Preece)
1933 (cat.49)
Oil on canvas, 763 × 637mm
Private collection

Children with toys
1933 (cat.50)
Oil on canvas, 760 × 763mm
Private collection

Downshire Hill garden
1934 (cat.51)
Oil on canvas, 740 × 1065mm
Private collection

Slipway, Jersey
1935 (cat.52)
Oil on panel, 442 × 342mm
Private collection

A vision of God in heaven
1946 (cat.62)
Pastel, 795 × 755mm
Private collection

Study for blind,
antique shop, Westminster
1939 (cat.55)
Gouache, 286 × 336mm
Private collection

CHRONOLOGY

1889 20 November: Annie Hilda Carline born in London, fourth of five children of George Carline (1855–1920) and Annie, née Smith (1862–1945).

c.1892 The family settles in Oxford at The Shrubbery, Woodstock Road.

c.1899 George Carline loses much of the family money in an unsuccessful business venture.

c.1899–1900 Residence at Neuchâtel, Switzerland.

c.1901–3 Residence at Repton, Derbyshire.

1903 Returns to Oxford, to 3 Park Crescent.

1903–8 Hilda attends Oxford High School. Wins many certificates for drawing and leaves with a Higher School Certificate in French, Maths, History and Biology.

1906 Hilda's brother Roland dies of tuberculosis.

1909–12 At home in Oxford, producing landscape, genre and portrait water-colours under father's guidance.

1913 With brothers Sydney and Richard joins Percyval Tudor-Hart's School of Painting in Maitland Villas, north London; living in a rented flat at 4 Downshire Hill, Hampstead.

1916 Joined the Land Army with Cora Stoop, friend and fellow student at the Tudor-Hart School. Works on a farm at Wangford, Suffolk. Parents move to 47 Downshire Hill, Hampstead.

1919 End of Land Army service. Returns to London to her parent's new home and paints *Return from the farm*.
Summer: begins five years' part-time study at Slade School.

1919 December: meets Stanley Spencer at a family dinner.

1920 April: Family painting holiday at Seaford, Sussex, joined by Stanley Spencer.
Summer: painting in the Italian Alps with Sydney and Richard, later joined by their parents.
November: Death of George Carline at Assisi as the family journeyed south to Rome.

1921 First exhibits with the London Group.

1922 Summer: painting holiday in Yugoslavia, joined by Stanley Spencer. He proposes to Hilda for the first time.

1923 Summer painting holiday in Andorra, Spain.

1924 Paints landscapes in Essex and Suffolk, where joined by Stanley.

1925 23 February: Marriage to Stanley in Wangford Parish Church. Honeymoon in Wangford. Return to London to live in the Vale of Health Hotel, Hampstead.
November: birth of first daughter, Shirin.

1927 May: the family move to a rented room at Palmer's Hill Farm, Burghclere, Hampshire.

1928 February: the family move into Chapel View Cottage. Elsie Munday becomes the family's maid.

1929 February: death of Sydney Carline from pneumonia.
Summer: family painting holiday in Cookham with Stanley, Shirin, Hilda's mother and brother Richard; Hilda paints again after a four year break.

1929 First meeting with Patricia Preece and Dorothy Hepworth.

1930 May: birth of second daughter, Unity.

1932 January: the family move to Lindworth, Cookham on Thames.
Beginning of relationship between Stanley and Patricia Preece.
Hilda in Hampstead nursing her brother George, seriously ill with heart disease.
December: death of George Carline.

1933 Living only intermittently at Cookham, otherwise in Hampstead.
Shirin living permanently with Mrs Harter at Prince Arthur's Road, Hampstead.
Summer: takes children to Wangford and paints *Children with toys*.
December: visits Cookham and paints portrait of Patricia Preece.

1934 May: separation from Stanley; living at 47 Downshire Hill, Hampstead. Paints *Downshire Hill garden*.
Autumn: holiday in Switzerland with Unity.
Summer: holiday in Jersey with mother and children.

1936 Initiates divorce proceedings.

1937 May: Decree Absolute declared. Stanley marries Patricia Preece.
Summer: moves to 17 Pond Street, Hampstead, the new Carline family home.
Visits Tossa, Spain

1938 Painting holiday in North Wales.

1939 Accompanies her mother to the opening of Annie Carline's exhibition at Galerie Pittoresque, Paris.
Unity joins Shirin living with Mrs Harter, now in Epsom.

1940 Shirin and Unity attend Badminton School, evacuated to Lynmouth, Devon.
Death of two close friends in the blitz, Constance Oliver and Eddie Pearson.

1942 June: Mental breakdown. Admitted to Banstead Hospital, Surrey and remains there nine months. Visited each week by Stanley.

1943 Draws *Children and nature* pastels. Moves to a room at 224 Finchley Road, under the care of psychiatrist Dr Brier.

1945 Returns to live at 17 Pond Street, Hampstead.

1946 Visit to Paris with Shirin and Richard Carline.

1947 Breast cancer diagnosed and mastectomy performed.

1950 1 November: Dies at Royal Free Hospital, Hampstead.

CATALOGUE

All measurements provided as
height × width in millimetres

HILDA CARLINE
1889–1950

1 *Flower seller*
1909–10
Water-colour on paper, 381 × 271mm
Private collection
Illustrated, p.12

2 *Head of an old man*
1909–10
Water-colour on paper, 392 × 285mm
Private collection
Illustrated, p.13

3 *Canal bridge*
*c.*1909
Water-colour on paper, 290 × 224mm
Private collection
Illustrated, p.12

4 *Study of trees*
*c.*1910
Pencil on paper, 382 × 278mm
Private collection

5 *Self-portrait*
1913
Water-colour on paper, 355 × 252mm
Private collection
Illustrated, p.8

6 *Bathing hut, Lincoln*
1914
Water-colour on paper, 191 × 275mm
Private collection
Illustrated, p.13

7 *A Fantasy*
1914
Oil on canvas, 382 × 485mm
Private collection
Illustrated, p.49

8 *Still-life with gold mirror and Buddha*
1914
Water-colour on paper, 253 × 175mm
Private collection
Illustrated, p.14

9 *Zeppelin over London*
1915
Oil on canvas, 225 × 225mm
Private collection
Illustrated, p.14

10 *Male nude*
1915
Pencil on paper, 445 × 287mm
Private collection

11 *Back view of a female nude*
1915
Pencil on paper, 382 × 276mm
Private collection
Illustrated, p.16

12 *Noah & the Ark*
1915
Water-colour on card, 207 × 204mm
Private collection

13 *Man in grey*
1915
Oil on canvas, 574 × 440mm
Private collection
Illustrated, p.14

14 *Standing male nude*
1916
Pencil on paper, 382 × 282mm
Private collection

15 *Harley Trotter dancing at his party*
1916
Water-colour on paper, 380 × 278mm
Private collection

16 *Two men fencing*
1916
Conté on paper, 317 × 508mm
Private collection

17 *Return from the farm*
1919
Oil on canvas, 1300 × 910mm
Private collection
Illustrated, p.50

18 *Bathing tents*
1920
Oil on canvas, 355 × 290mm
Private collection

19 *Cliffs, Seaford*
1920
Oil on canvas, 1102 × 622mm
Private collection
Illustrated, p.51

20 *Self-portrait*
1920
Conté on paper, 260 × 200mm
Signed, lower right 'Hilda Carline/ June 1920'
Inscribed lower left 'For Competition'
Private collection

21 *The artist's mother*
1920
Pencil on paper, 386 × 276mm
Inscribed, lower right (by a later hand?) 'Her mother by Hilda Carline *c.*1920'
Private collection

22 *Hillside, Assisi*
1920
Water-colour on paper, 280 × 378mm
Private collection
Illustrated, p.52

23 *Count Tossa's children*
1921
Oil on canvas, 1285 × 865mm
Signed, lower right 'Hilda Carline/1920'
Private collection
Illustrated, p.53

24 *Lake Orta*
1920
Oil on canvas, 420 × 555mm
Signed, lower right 'Hilda Carline/1920'
Private collection
Illustrated, p.52

25 *Melancholy in a country garden*
1921
Oil on canvas, 660 × 698mm
Private collection
Illustrated, p.32

26 *Richard Carline painting at Steep*
1921
Water-colour on paper, 272 × 217mm
Inscribed, upper right (by a later hand) 'By Hilda Carline. Dick painting at Steep/1921/Design for a woodcut'
Private collection

27 *Standing female nude*
1922
Oil on canvas, 750 × 500mm
Signed, verso 'H. Carline'
Private collection
Illustrated, p.54

28 *Standing male nude, back view*
1922
Oil on canvas, 763 × 505mm
Private collection

29 *Woman in a red hat*
1922
Oil on canvas, 606 × 480mm
Signed, lower right 'H. Carline/1922'
Private collection
Illustrated, p.54

30 *Female nude*
1922
Pencil on paper, 367 × 266mm
Private collection

31 *Group study: male nudes*
1922
Pencil on paper, 560 × 381mm
Private collection

32 *Group study: female nudes*
1922
Pencil on paper, 560 × 378mm
Private collection

33 *Wooden minaret*
1922
Oil on canvas, 380 × 293mm
Private collection
Illustrated, p.55

34 *Donkeys, Sarajevo*
1922
Oil on canvas, 292 × 292mm
Private collection
Illustrated, p.55

35 *Street scene, Sarajevo*
1922
Oil on canvas, 220 × 347mm
Private collection

36 *Waterfall, Mostar*
1922
Oil on canvas, 554 × 445mm
Signed, lower left 'Hilda Carline/1922'
Private collection
Illustrated, p.21

37 *Mending nets*
1922
Oil on paper, laid down on card, 241 × 305mm
Private collection

38 *Portrait of Stanley Spencer*
1923
Oil on canvas, 610 × 458mm
Private collection
Illustrated, p.56

39 *Self-portrait*
1923
Oil on canvas, 749 × 578mm
Tate Gallery, London
Illustrated, Cover and p.57

40 *Wangford*
1924
Water-colour on paper, 197 × 280mm
Private collection

41 *Smoke from the Southwold train, Wangford*
1925
Oil on canvas, 335 × 865mm
Private collection
Illustrated, p.58

42 *Miss Silcox*
1925
Pencil on paper, 354 × 253mm
Private collection
Illustrated, p.25

43 *Elsie*
1929
Oil on canvas, 1727 × 813mm
The Brighton and Hove Collections
Illustrated, p.59

44 *The fireplace*
1929
Oil on canvas mounted on board, 355 × 270mm
Private collection

45 *Swans, Cookham Bridge*
c.1929
Oil on canvas, 380 × 766mm
Royal Academy 1935 (499)
Harris Museum & Art Gallery, Preston
Illustrated, Back cover

46 *Portrait of the artist's mother*
1930
Oil on canvas, 710 × 610mm
Private collection
Illustrated, p.31

47 *Stanley nude*
1931
Pencil on paper, 508 × 353mm
Signed, upper right 'Hilda Carline 1931'
Scottish National Gallery of Modern Art, Edinburgh
Illustrated, p.34

48 *Portrait of Shirin*
1931
Oil on panel, 420 × 317mm
Private collection
Illustrated, p.32

49 *Lady in green (portrait of Patricia Preece)*
1933
Oil on canvas, 763 × 637mm
Signed, lower right 'Hilda Carline 1933'
Private collection
Illustrated, p.60

50 *Children with toys*
1933
Oil on canvas, 760 × 763mm
Signed, lower left 'Hilda Carline. 1933'
Royal Academy 1936 (497)
Private collection
Illustrated, p.61

51 *Downshire Hill garden*
1934
Oil on canvas, 740 × 1065mm
Private collection
Illustrated, p.62

52 *Slipway, Jersey*
1935
Oil on panel, 442 × 342mm
Signed 'Hilda Carline 1935'
Private collection
Illustrated, p.63

53 *Portrait of Unity*
1937
Oil on board, 534 × 428mm
Signed, lower right 'Hilda Carline/ 1937'
Private collection
Illustrated, p.43

54 *Luxembourg Gardens, Paris*
1939
Oil on canvas, 597 × 727mm
Signed, lower left 'Hilda Carline 1939'
Private collection
Illustrated, p.45

55 *Study for blind, antique shop, Westminster*
1939
Gouache on black paper, 286 × 336mm
Private collection
Illustrated, p.64

56 *Wartime gardens, Hampstead*
1943
Oil on canvas, 560 × 660mm
Signed, lower left 'Hilda Carline 1943'
Royal Academy 1944 (246)
Private collection

57 *Winter; study for mural*
c.1943
Pastel on paper, 365 × 665mm
Private collection

58 *The seasons; study for mural*
c.1943
Pastel on paper, 400 × 672mm
Private collection

59 *Children and nature: study for a mural*
c.1943
Pastel on paper, 150 × 180mm
Private collection
Illustrated, p.45

60 *A boulevard in Paris*
1946
Oil on canvas, 355 × 268mm
Private collection
Illustrated, p.46

61 *Luxembourg Gardens, Paris*
1946
Oil on canvas, 550 × 460mm
Signed, lower right 'Hilda Carline/ 1946'
Private collection

62 *A vision of God in heaven*
1946
Pastel on paper, 495 × 755mm
Private collection
Illustrated, p.64

GEORGE CARLINE
1855–1920

63 *Red admiral*
1904
Water-colour on paper, 297 × 215mm
Signed, left 'George Carline/1904'
Private collection
Illustrated, p.11

SYDNEY CARLINE
1888–1929

64 *Portrait of Hilda*
*c.*1913
Pencil on paper, 362 × 285mm
Private collection
Illustrated, p.11

RICHARD CARLINE
1896–1980

65 *Portrait of Hilda Carline*
1918
Oil on canvas, 762 × 635mm
Signed, lower right 'Richard Carline 1918'
Tate Gallery, London
Illustrated, p.15

66 *Gathering on the terrace*
1925
Oil on canvas, 1950 × 1613mm
Ferens Art Gallery, Kingston upon Hull
Illustrated, p.23

STANLEY SPENCER
1891–1959

67 *Sarajevo*
1922
Oil on canvas, 360 × 253mm
South London Art Gallery
Illustrated, p.21

68 *Hilda*
1928
Pencil on paper, 357 × 254mm
The Visitors of the Ashmolean Museum, Oxford

69 *Hilda nude*
1931
Pencil on paper, 508 × 352mm
Scottish National Gallery of Modern Art, Edinburgh
Illustrated, p.34

70 *Hilda, Unity and dolls*
1937
Oil on canvas, 762 × 508mm
City Art Gallery, Leeds
Illustrated, p.41

71 *Marriage at Cana*
1953
Oil on canvas, 660 × 501mm
Glynn Vivian Art Gallery, Swansea
Illustrated, p.46

GILBERT SPENCER
1892–1979

72 *Portrait of Hilda*
1925
Pencil on paper, 295 × 177mm
Inscribed, lower left 'Hilda/G. Spencer/1925'
Private collection
Illustrated, p.25

SELECT BIBLIOGRAPHY

BOOKS

Bell, Keith, *Stanley Spencer: A Complete Catalogue of the Paintings*, Phaidon Press, London, 1992

Carline, Richard, *Stanley Spencer at War*, Faber and Faber Ltd, London, 1978

MacCarthy, Fiona, *Stanley Spencer: An English Vision*, Yale University Press, London, 1997

Pople, Kenneth, *Stanley Spencer: A Biography*, Collins, London, 1991

Rothenstein, Sir John, ed., *Stanley Spencer: The Man, Correspondence and Reminiscences*, Paul Elek, London, 1979

Spencer, Gilbert *Stanley Spencer by his brother, Gilbert*, Victor Gollancz, London, 1961

EXHIBITION CATALOGUES

The Spencers and Carlines in Hampstead in the 1920s, Stanley Spencer Gallery, Cookham, 1973

Stanley and Hilda Spencer, with an introduction by Richard Carline, Anthony d'Offay Gallery, London, 1978

Stanley Spencer RA, Keith Bell, with contributions from Richard Carline and Andrew Causey, Royal Academy, London, 1980

Richard Carline, with an essay by Elizabeth Cowling, Camden Arts Centre, London, 1983

Images of Hilda Spencer, Stanley Spencer Gallery, Cookham, 1985

Stanley Spencer: a Hampstead Vision, Burgh House, London, 1991

Stanley Spencer: The Apotheosis of Love, with an introduction by Jane Alison and an essay by Timothy Hyman, Barbican Art Gallery, London, 1991

CREDITS AND ACKNOWLEDGEMENTS

The organisers wish to thank all those who have lent works to the exhibition and also: The Arts Council of England; Janet Balmforth; The late Mrs E. Beckford; Adrian Buckley; Nancy Carline; Courtauld Institute of Art Photographic Survey; Jane Cunningham; Michael Dickens; Rachel Duffield, DACS; John Gill; Adrian Glew, Tate Gallery Archive; Dave Gribbin; Jane Martineau; Kenneth Pople; John Ross and Frances Spalding.

The organisers are grateful to Shirin and Unity Spencer, for permission to quote from correspondence held by the Tate Gallery Archive; for permission to reproduce family photographs and works by Stanley Spencer and Hilda Carline and for their generous support and encouragement at every stage.

Photographs are supplied by the owners and by Bridgeman Art Library London/New York; Walter Gardner, Worthing; Sotheby's, London; and the Witt Library, Courtauld Institute of Art, London. *Return from the farm*: photograph by John Parker; *Smoke from the Southwold train, Wangford*: photograph by Jean McAlpine.